BDSM Mastery— Relationships
a guide for creating mindful relationships for Dominants and submissives

by Robert J. Rubel Ph.D.

and

M. Jen Fairfield

Other Books by Robert J. Rubel

Master/slave Relations: Handbook of Theory and Practice
> This book was totally revised and is now available as: *Master/slave Mastery: Updated handbook of concepts, approaches, and practices* by Robert J. Rubel and M. Jen Fairfield (2014

Protocols Handbook for the Leather slave: Theory and Practice
> (This is the gender-neutral version of Protocols: Handbook for the Female slave.) More than a book of traditional Leather protocols, this book demonstrates how to use protocols to make your particular relationship magical. This book is intended to suggest protocols that you, yourself, will adapt to your particular structure.

Master/slave Relations: Communications 401–the advanced course
> All relationships have communication challenges, and many of these challenges are amplified when living in a structured relationship. This book teases out some of communication glitches that are often hard to identify and modify even in vanilla relationships. This book is written specifically for couples living in a D/s or M/s structure where there are certain constraints when speaking with one another.

Master/slave Relations: Solutions 402–living in harmony
> If you're sensing that one of you is growing apart from the other, if you are concerned that one or more of your core values may be different from your partner and you want to work on growing back together, this is your book. It's really a book of things to think/talk about that will strengthen your relationship.

All published by Nazca Plains, Las Vegas, Nevada. You can purchase these books through Amazon.

Signed copies are available directly from Jen and Dr. Bob through their website, *www.KinkMastery.com*

Dear Readers –

This is the second in our series of books on BDSM Mastery. The first book in this series is titled: *BDSM Mastery--Basics: your guide to play, parties, and scene protocols* and if you've not yet read that book I highly recommend it as a basic understanding of this culture.

If you have read the first book in this series, you will find some of that material repeated here for the benefit of those who are reading this book without having first read the *BDSM Mastery-- Basics* book. Not only is this information important for both books but is also needed to repeat it here to give a context for this material on D/s relationships.

This is a book about relationships. Adventuresome relationships. Relationships that are not exactly like *vanilla* relationships. BDSM relationships differ in two specific ways from your typical vanilla relationship: first, they usually involve a *power-imbalanced* structure (one person is clearly in charge and the other person is clearly following); second, the kind of sex that adventuresome folks practice is, well, *not vanilla.*

I wrote this book to help you better to understand the power dynamics that get involved with what are called *power- imbalanced* relationships (usually referred to as Dominant/ submissive or D/s relationships).

While we make a distinction between *power-imbalanced* relationships and *authority-transfer* relationships, I will touch on Master/slave (M/s) and Owner/property (O/p) relationships in this book.

I have learned a great deal about BDSM and Master/slave material since my last books in the 2006-7 period. I hope you enjoy the differences.

– Robert J. (Dr. Bob) Rubel

Acknowledgements

There are a select few other people who have gone out of their way to help make this book what it has become and I owe each of them a deep debt of gratitude:

- **PhoenixRed** (her scene name on Fet) holds a Ph.D. both in Psychology and in Neural Science and has been active in the local Kansas City area BDSM community since 2006. She has poured her heart and soul into two complete readings of this book, once to make substantive comments and once to conduct a complete editorial review. This is no trivial matter, and I am grateful beyond words for the breadth of experience and balance she has brought to this work. Thanks, Phoenix, you've made a difference.

- **Dan** (AngelRiot on Fet) asked to read this book and offered to critique it. I had thought that I was finished with it, but once I started reading his notes, I realized that I still had a *lot* more work to do. Dan, thank you for your thoughtful comments. I believe that I took them all.

- **Sir_Dragon_Z** (his name on Fet, from Victoria, B.C., Canada) was one of the final readers. His thoughtful comments about D/s relationships helped make a number of important sections of this book far richer than they would otherwise have been. Outgoing and gregarious, Sir Dragon's subtle observations frequently surprise me. Even while standing and speaking with him, I frequently find myself reaching for my notebook in order to capture his ideas. "Wait, wait," I'll say, "What did you just say?" Thanks B., you're a gem!

Other Books by Robert J. Rubel and M. Jen Fairfield

BDSM Mastery—Basics: your guide to play, parties, and scene protocols (Book One in the BDSM Mastery Series)
2014

Master/slave Mastery: updated handbook of concepts, approaches, and practices (Book One in the Master/slave Mastery Series)
2014

Master/slave Mastery: Refining the fire—ideas that matter (Book Two in the Master/slave Mastery Series)
2015

Books are published by Red Eight Ball Press, Austin, TX and signed copies are available through *www.KinkMastery.com* or through Amazon.

BDSM Mastery— Relationships
a guide for creating mindful relationships for Dominants and submissives

by Robert J. Rubel Ph.D.

and

M. Jen Fairfield

www.KinkMastery.com

Red Eight Ball Press
P.O. Box 171303
Austin, TX 78717

BDSM Mastery—Relationships
a guide for creating mindful relationships
for Dominants and submissives

Cover Design: M. Jen Fairfield and RhodesCreativeStudio
Cover Photo: Out of the Night
Cover Photographer: Robert J. Rubel
Photo Model: Don and Nova

Library of Congress Catalog Number: 2014960027

Published by Red Eight Ball Press
Printed in the United States of America

Dedicated to the brave kinky explorers who passed on what they learned so that we who follow them can explore even further.

Preface

I love writing books. The process helps me solidify my own knowledge. This is the second in our series of books on BDSM Mastery. The first book in this series is titled: *BDSM Mastery—Basics: your guide to play, parties, and scene protocols*. If you have not yet read that book, I recommend it to you, for it will give you a thorough understanding of (and appreciation for) the overall background of the BDSM culture in which BDSM relationships thrive. The next book in this series will be on BDSM sex. Our working title is: *BDSM Mastery—Sex: your guide for erotically adventuresome nights*.

Since discovering the world of BDSM in 2001, I've spent a lot of time reading, writing, and thinking about this culture. As interest in BDSM has recently exploded, books and Websites have sprung up offering countless thousands of facts and opinions about it. Some of this material is superb, but other material wanders between *sort of right but too superficial* through the land of *maybe, but not in my experience* to the quicksand of *who in the world made this up*?

My Ph.D. is in educational sociology; since 2006, I've been writing books and doing demos and presentations at BDSM conferences worldwide. I've led well over 200 classes and workshops, and since Fall, 2012 my co-author and I have been conducting free hour-long twice-monthly webinars on various BDSM topics. Over this time I've learned to identify when BDSM material is generally accurate or a little *off*.

I wrote this book to help you better to understand the power dynamics that get involved with what are called *power-imbalanced* relationships—relationships where someone is clearly leading and someone is clearly following.

By the time you finish the book, you'll know quiet a bit about...
- Personal, sexual, and sado-masochistic roles you can explore,
- Suggestions for finding a partner and establishing a good fit with that person,
- Emotional safety, and
- Many things to consider as a couple

By the way, I've included an extensive glossary of BDSM terms in the Supplements. You might want to scan over it before you begin reading the book: it will help you understand words and phrases that are not part of your usual vocabulary.

Most important, by the end of this book you'll be able to identify partners who will be good for you.

Personal biases

I write in first person present tense so that I can speak with you directly (I dislike academic prose). Also, I write in spirals, so if you think you've already heard me say something, chances are you did. I do this in order to lay down one layer of ideas upon which I can then add other layers of more complex ideas.

I follow the common BDSM writing convention of referring to people who are filling the role of the submissive partner as a *sub* and if a personal name of a sub is to be mentioned, the first letter of that sub's name will be in lowercase.

Carrying this thought a bit further, I've endeavored to keep this book gender-neutral. Rather than *Dom*, I write it as *Dom/me*—a combination of the abbreviation for a male dominant (Dom) and a female dominant (Domme, also pronounced as Dom). Similarly, as bottoms (those on the receiving end of BDSM play) may be either male or female, I avoid referring to them as *subs* or *she*, favoring *they* or *them*, as in: *The*

Dom/me may instruct them to do X, rather than say: *The Dom may instruct her to do X*.

I will sometimes use the term "D-type" to refer to dominants of any gender and the term "s-type" to refer to submissives or slaves of either gender. Top/bottom is about the physical body; Dom/sub is about the mental body; Master/slave is about the spiritual body (credit to Master Steve Sampson and Master Skip Chasey many years ago for so clearly explaining these terms). Seldom, but a few times in this book, I'll refer to a *Master* as distinct from a Dom/me. When you are first starting out, there is a lot of confusion between the words *Master* and *Dom*. When I use *Master* it will be for a particular reason—explained in a general way in the Glossary (Supplement A).

I'm writing this way because very little in the world of BDSM actually depends on gender or orientation and I'm endeavoring to break you right now of the cultural habits that can get you in trouble in this culture. People generally think that Doms are male and submissives are female. It's not that clean-cut in reality.

Personal biases that influence my writing
I have some personal biases you should be aware of.

I am pro-women and anti-macho and pro-learning/practice and anti-improvisation. While it can be lots of fun to play Tarzan and Jane during a scene (hope you're not too young to get that reference!), I'm concerned that—in the excitement of their newly discovered world—Tarzan may overlook some of Jane's needs for support and encouragement in the non-BDSM parts of their lives.

I believe that it's important for Tarzan's and Jane's BDSM activities to augment their sexual and intellectual growth. Otherwise

"Everyone in BDSM starts at the same place. Where they end up is a function of their interests and the choices they make along the way."

--*Mindi*, my former slave of eight years

they risk reinforcing a stereotype of male-Dominant BDSM: "Me Tarzan, Jane my property! Jane do as I say or me beat Jane!" Oh, and a safety tip for Tarzan: Be sure your rope is secured correctly before trying to swing into our community.

The companion book to this book is:

BDSM Mastery— Basics: your guide to play, parties, and scene protocols.

That book is about Tops and bottoms;
This book is about Dom/mes and submissives.

Once you *swing in*, you're going to find BDSM a world of mind-bending combinations and contradictions. This book, the first in the *BDSM Mastery* series, is intended to demystify this world without draining any of the excitement.

About my co-author
Despite the book's first-person-singular style, M. Jen Fairfield influenced virtually every section either directly or indirectly. I could not have written it without her constant influence in my life. That is why she is listed as co-author: She earned the position.

For those who are curious—and particularly those who see us at conferences—I'll say up front that Jen is 20 years younger than me and had no prior BDSM experience before we began dating in March 2010. However, during our years together, her continual questions, her probing, and her wide-ranging kinky interests have spurred me to do more and more research about BDSM—in part to satisfy her nearly insatiable mind.

Thanks to Jen's influence in my life, *BDSM Mastery* is quite different from my previous books on Master/slave relationships. Born in 1944, I grew up during the height of the Cold War, when Kennedy was President and my father worked as a senior official at the Pentagon. Jen was born when Kennedy was President and came of age as a hippie. My earlier books lack her influence, and those who have read (or will read) them will be struck by that difference.

Perhaps the best reason why Jen is credited as the co-author is that the book simply wouldn't have taken the same shape, texture, or tone without her.

Oh – one last thought: *please be patient*, both in BDSM and in reading this book. Rushing forward blindly rarely ends well. Even if your eyes glaze over reading pages in which I carefully analyze key terms and concepts, sooner or later you'll find every bit of this book relevant to finding your way in the BDSM world, where little details can quickly become *big* issues.

— *Robert J. Rubel* Austin, Texas 2014

Table of Contents

Introduction

Chapter 3: Finding a Partner

Chapter 4: Roles Within Relationships

Table of Contents

Supplements

Introduction

This is the second book in a series on BDSM: Bondage/discipline; Dominance and submission; sado-masochism.

The previous book discussed the culture of BDSM—what it is and how you can fit in safely. That book focused on the physical aspects of *SM (sado-masochistic) play*. I kept discussions about *relationships* out of that first book because the topic is too complex to have included it: this entire book addresses power exchange relationships (usually referred to as Dominant/submissive or D/s relationships).

Now—I have written this book assuming that you have already read the prior book. That means that I assume you know how important it is to master your physical SM skills, how your reputation in our community depends upon your honor and integrity, and that when you're *playing*, you're using *safewords* and playing according to SSC standards (**S**afe, **S**ane, and **C**onsensual). If you have *not* read the other book, you may find that I allude to material in this book that doesn't quite make sense to you.

Occasionally in this book I'll touch on Master/slave (M/s) and Owner/property (O/p) relationships, but this is not the book for those topics, either. M/s and O/p relationships are based on *authority transfer* and they differ from D/s relationships in many fundamental ways. If you think that you may be interested in M/s or O/p relationships, I refer you to my four-book set:
- *Master/slave Relations: Handbook of Theory and Practice* (2006)
- *Protocol Handbook for the Leather Slave: Theory and Practice* (2006)
- *Master/slave Relations: Communications 401—The Advanced Course* (2007)
- *Master/slave Relations: Solutions 402—Living in Harmony* (2007)

Introduction

I expect that by the end of 2014 that my fully revised and updated version of that first book will be available; I expect to have updated the Protocols book by Spring 2015. You can do an Amazon search on *Master/slave Mastery* to check new titles. Oh: and you can also search on *BDSM Mastery* to see whether new books are out in this series, as well.

But, this is a book about relationships. Adventuresome relationships. Relationships that are not exactly like *vanilla* relationships—traditional relationships as practiced by the average person you'd meet at a baseball game. BDSM relationships differ in two specific ways: first, they usually involve a power-imbalanced structure (one person is clearly in charge and the other person is clearly following); second, the kind of sex that adventuresome folks practice is, well, *not vanilla*. I'll get into that a bit later, but—frankly—that was the focus of the first book in this series.

And, there are other reasons for reading this book.

You'll want to read/master the material in this book once the newness of the BDSM world starts to wear off and your interest is piqued about how one can incorporate more of this lifestyle into your own life.

You'll want to read/master this material when you find a play partner that you like and who seems to like you and you're thinking of getting to know them better.

You'll want to have read/mastered this material if you're thinking of starting a relationship with someone as adventuresome as yourself.

Chapter 1
Short, Basic Orientation to Kink

BDSM? Kinky sex? Play/Scene Relationships?

You may wish to incorporate some kind of a relationship with your kinky play. Then again, you may not. Or, you may wish to have a kinky relationship without kinky play.

Maybe you'll be play partners; maybe there will be some form of dominance and submission. Before we discuss options within a power-imbalanced structure, lets talk a little about being kinky, just to be sure that we're both talking the same language.

The letters *BDSM* represent an open-ended range of practices and expressions—including many forms of restraint, sensory stimulation, role-playing, and interpersonal dynamics. These activities are usually erotic at some level but might not involve genital intercourse. *BDSM* derives from a combination of the letters *B and D*, for bondage and discipline (corporal punishment), and the letters *S and M* (also S/M or SM) for sadism and masochism (or sado-masochism). SM typically involves pain and/or humiliation. Fairly recently people noticed that the letters *D* and *S* in the middle can stand for Dominance and submission (D/s), so those letters are now incorporated into the overall explanation of the acronym *BDSM*.

"i am an active lifestyle participant in BDSM. It is not a lifestyle for everyone, and not everyone who is a part of the lifestyle necessarily participates in a 24/7 BDSM life. Some people save it just for the weekends, or even just once a month."

— *kerin*, Yahoo Answers

Since both bondage and discipline and sado-masochism usually involve at least temporary dominance by one person over another (who submits to the former's control), most people in the BDSM world now view it as a kind of three-ring circus where participants either can move around or stay focused on just one or two rings.

For some, BDSM is about authority-based relationships—the giving or receiving of service that may or may not be sexual. For others, BDSM is about intensifying their sexual relations. For still others, BDSM is about losing themselves temporarily in intense sensations or unusual psychological states—even spiritual ones—resulting from bondage or pain play. Of course, there are also the edgy few who are drawn to pain-centered SM practices simply because they are so taboo within the mainstream culture. Moths to flames, as it were.

Common Misconceptions about BDSM

Interest in BDSM can range from a one-time experiment to a complete change in your style of living. For some, oral sex is kinky; for others, it's as normal as breathing. For some, spanking during sex is kinky; for others, it just adds some interest to regular sexual play. For some, having clearly defined authority roles and consequences tied to actions seems ultra-conservative and outdated; for others, it provides a stable and understandable relationship framework.

People seldom question things that they think we *know* to be true; things we think are true remain largely invisible to us. Actually, it seldom occurs to us that we even *can* question them. After life-long exposure to culturally-accepted conditions, our subconscious often stores this information as *fact*. As an example, when we see someone doing something that our culture has labeled *taboo*, our subconscious minds pair that incoming information with other subconscious memories and—voila! a stereotypical opinion takes hold of us and we react (usually negatively). Our unstable realities are built upon the shifting sands of what we can recall of our experiences. Unless we are careful, we can easily find ourselves filtering our reactions through culturally accepted reactions instead of through our own truths.

Beyond cultural bias, misconceptions can arise for many reasons:
- Our conclusions were based on incomplete or misunderstood facts.
- Our brains reinterpreted what we saw and fit it to what we already knew—often resulting in conclusions based on our cultural background and personal experiences.
- We projected our personal reactions on to others: we believed that if *we* were in xyz situation *we* would behave in a certain way therefore others who are in xyz situation must think/behave that way or we question their motivations and intent.
- Sometimes, we make gross generalizations in order to distance ourselves from some topic. We generalize something in order to avoid having to learn enough about it to challenge what we are so sure we already know.

Here are some examples of large-scale misconceptions in the vanilla world:
- If you work hard, you'll succeed.
- Gay males are effeminate.
- Cross-dressers are gay
- Homeless people are basically different (less competent) than you and me or they wouldn't be homeless.
- Masochists enjoy all kinds of pain regardless of the type or context.
- Sadists get off on making people suffer, whether or not their victim has consented.

Examples of large-scale misconceptions **within** the BDSM community (provided by Master Arach for use in this book) include:
- A submissive female is a girl who doesn't understand feminism.

- A submissive male lacks masculinity.
- A dominant female needs to be cheered on: *You go, girl.*
- A dominant male (or female) who plays heavily is an abuser.

Examples of common *outsider* misconceptions **about** BDSM include:
- The BDSM culture is just about pain.
- You should call a dominant woman *Mistress*.
- If you're a slave/submissive, you must obey any Dominant or Master.
- The point of female domination is to keep the male from feeling pleasure or satisfaction.
- A dominant that switches is less of a dominant than those who don't switch.
- A submissive who switches is less of a submissive than those who don't switch.
- Dominants are superior to submissives as human beings.
- Switches need both to Top and to bottom to feel satisfied.
- Bisexuals need male and female partners to feel satisfied.
- Before you can be a Dominant or a Master you must first experience serving as a submissive or slave.
- Before you use a toy you have to have it used on you.
- Being penetrated is inherently submissive; if a man wants to be penetrated anally but isn't interested in submitting, he is wrong.
- Men who like receiving anal sex are submissive and/or a little bit gay; women who like to penetrate men anally are dominant.
- It's never okay for submissives to approach Dominants at gatherings; it's never okay for submissives to ask for play.
- It's okay for Dominants to touch, command, manhandle or disrespect someone as long as their target is a submissive.
- And on and on and on.

Misconceptions can lead those unused to BDSM to feel disgusted, frightened, or simply disturbed by many of the ideas and actions that are supposedly accepted within BDSM circles. This book is designed to help give you the additional insights and ideas to enable you to draw your own conclusions about your possible participation with BDSM and kinky relationships.

BDSM encompasses a wide field

Please realize that the general term *BDSM* includes people with a wide, wide range of interests and kinky preferences. Each have their own ways of interacting with one another that are too broad to cover in this book; practically every sentence would have to be qualified. So—I've taken a lot of trouble to present a broad range of material that is generally true of most BDSM practitioners.

Since you are reading this book, I am assured that BDSM interests you. The thing of it is: the world of alternative sexuality is a real, live culture in the sociological sense of the term. That is, those of us who participate actively in the various BDSM communities share a general set of attitudes, values, goals, and practices. These rules, standards of behavior, and symbols have to be learned a little bit at a time.

Complexity

By the time you've had a few good (and safe) BDSM experiences, you'll also find that you have a LOT of studying and listening and asking to do in order to understand the rules, values, and expectations of this culture. You'll realize that it is not one single culture, but a collection of subcultures that have some common elements and some important differences. You'll find that *littles* live here next to *spankos* who cock an eyebrow at BDSM players who are viewed with a certain caution by *Leatherfolk*. And then there are the *Goreans, fuzzies, pony players, pets,* and *Daddies with their boys* and *Daddies with their bois*, let alone *Daddies with their little girls* that—by the way—are very different than *Daddies with their daughters*. Most of these groups have different foci, rules, and customs. Oh, and just wait until you encounter a dominant who insist that there is no inconsistency in being a slave.

It's going to take you some time—possibly years—to wrap your head around all this.

Because this can be a risky path to walk, those of us who have been living this way for a while try to get newcomers to slow down. "Take your time," we say: "Go to classes. Find a mentor. Don't get hooked up with the first Dom or sub that wants to have a relationship with you."

In my experience, though, hormones (and/or the excitement of very new things) take over early in a relationship and the newcomers ignore such advice. Jumping into the ocean can cause you to get your feelings hurt; you can get your body hurt. At the worst, you can become psychologically damaged. Take small steps and master the step before you move forward. You not only have your own well-being to consider, you have the well-being of the person you are playing with or the person you are embarking on a relationship with. I'm just sayin'...

I'm not sure that I'm kinky, why would I be interested in BDSM?

Well, I'm 70, but my reply to that question is quite clear: Life is short. BDSM is an unusual Path. In my humble opinion, the BDSM path much more interesting than the alternative—being vanilla. Personally, if being offered ice cream, I 'd like to be able sample some flavors that are beyond vanilla. In sex and in relationships, that brings you to BDSM.

Remember that we just went over some misconceptions about BDSM? Well, you may have the misconception that BDSM necessarily involves SM play: floggers, spanking, bondage. Not so. You can be kinky in terms of your sexual play alone, you can be kinky in terms of your relationship structure alone, or you can be kinky in terms of your relationship structure that includes kinky sexual play (admittedly the most common form for BDSMers).

Let me run that one by you again.

BDSM covers a wide swath of ground. I've already said that. Sure, it covers physical SM play. Sure, it covers psychological play. Sure, it covers role play. So, by extrapolation, BDSM—the world of kinky folks—would cover couples who live in role play whether or not they engage in SM play. "Wow!" you might say. "Do you mean that they have *vanilla* sex but life 24/7 in some kind of role play? How does that work.

Well, stay tuned. Personally, I lived for 8 years as Master to a slave and if we had an SM play scene once a year I'd be surprised. It wasn't our "thing." Our "thing" was dressing up in gorgeous fetish attire and having formal dinners. Our "thing" was ceremony, not SM.
Pretty weird, right?

So "kinky" covers a lot of ground and this book is about the part of that ground that concerns dominance and submission in relationships.

On assumptions: some gentle warnings

Just because you see two people together at a kink event...

You have grown up in America. This is a good thing. But all cultures have their own ways of looking at the world, and in America family structures are *assumed* to be male-led (not that they all are, of course, it's just that people will assume that the man is running the household unless told otherwise). In patriarchal cultural models (where inheritance and lineage are traced through males), men are expected to be the dominant partner leading the relationship and women are expected (to a greater or lesser degree) to defer to and to serve their partner.

While many BDSM relationships mirror the tradition of male-led partnerships, quite a few do not. And, whether male or female led, most BDSM-based relationships are far more complex and flexible than relationships found in the larger U.S. society. It will take you a while to appreciate the rich variety of possible relationship options; right now, I'm just letting you know that they're out there.

In large part, because nobody knows who you are, how much education you have, or the kind of work you do unless you tell them, the BDSM community supports and encourages people to explore their personal identities. This is a world where the high-pressure executive can assume a submissive persona without being ridiculed. This is the world where a woman can express her dominance without being called a bitch. This is a world where a Master can be of either gender just as a slave can be of either gender. (Jen points out: a bitch *expects* service while a female dominant—just as a male dominant—*accepts* service in the context of her role as the dominant leader.)

It can be challenging to overcome our cultural biases: I get it. However, when you are meeting a couple for the first time I strongly recommend that you do *not* assume that the male is the dominant person in the relationship; roles can be fluid. Someone filling the role of a Dominant at one stage of their life may decide to explore their submissive side at another stage. While it is uncommon, I know of a case where after six years, the Master and slave changed roles. As I said: uncommon, but it happens.

When you meet someone...
To avoid creating an uncomfortable situation, you're going to want to ask others about the relationship status of the person/people you are interested in meeting before making assumptions about them. While the vast majority of relationships are Dom/sub, some relationships are Dom/Domme while others are Dom/switch or even switch/switch. If you are meeting a Dom/switch couple, you're not going to know whether the switch is in Dom/me or sub mode. So you have to ask. (I'm not making this up to be difficult: my personal relationship is Domme/switch. Sometimes I'm at public events as a Dom and sometimes I'm at public events in service to my Domme. It depends. Yes, people tell us that it confuses them.)

Of course, sometimes a person will advertise their status by what they're wearing—rather like wearing a wedding ring. In our culture, when an s-type belongs to a D-type, they often wear a collar. (I'll be discussing collars in depth in Chapter 4.) However, not *all* s-types wear collars—particularly if the submissive is a man. Please be slow to draw conclusions about someone's BDSM role based upon what they're wearing around their neck. Because there are no BDSM symbol police to control the meaning of personal attire/jewelry, what may scream *slave collar* to you may be something quite different to the wearer.
   • Wearing a collar does not make the person a submissive.

- What you think is only a necklace may, in fact, be a disguised collar (the person may have a job that requires wearing a discrete collar in public).
- What you think is a collar may only be that person's idea of a pretty necklace.
- What you are pretty sure is a BDSM collar may, in fact, be a BDSM collar.

Sometimes a cigar is a cigar, sometimes a cigar is a dildo, and sometimes a cigar is part of a fire play scene. You have to understand context.

If you are a dominant man and you are meeting a couple for the first time, your cultural training calls for you to offer your hand to the man—who is presumably the dominant partner. *In a BDSM setting, you may not wish to do this.* In the first place, you are assuming that the *man* is the D-type—and, as I just said, that might not be the case. In the second place, if you are new to the scene and the other person is established in the scene, you risk revealing how little you know of BDSM protocols if you start babbling on into an introduction that is not your place to make; wait for the more senior person to guide the conversation. If it is the woman who starts the conversation then you have a good idea she is the Domme. If she wishes to shake your hand she will extend hers to you.

Not to be too jarring, let me caution you that touching someone else's property is not tolerated. As in: you are not at liberty to shake the hand of someone's human property. While everyone understands normal politeness, BDSM relationships are usually more intense than boyfriend/

Sometimes a cigar is a cigar,
Sometimes a cigar is a dildo,
Sometimes a cigar is part of a fire play scene.

You have to understand context.

---

girlfriend relationships and the *no touching* restriction extends from *things* such as floggers to *people* such as a Dom's submissive—of either gender. When in doubt, ask. (Note: Unfortunately, online BDSMers often seem to ignore such common courtesies.)

Continuing for just a moment with the *touching* theme, let me address *hugging.*

Hugging is a form of intimacy. If you don't know the person very well, don't try hugging them. Similarly, if you are thinking of hugging someone and you are their junior (in terms of scene seniority) *don't do it.* It's just *too* vanilla and now your *touching* someone without having negotiated that level of intimacy. Folks who hug one another upon greeting or leaving are friends. It's not indiscriminate.

If it appears that someone is about to hug you and that's not okay with you, stick out your hand before the embrace takes hold. Trust me, they'll get the message.

When you address someone...

Because you can't (don't dare) identify everyone's BDSM role simply by his or her gender and clothing, it can be challenging to figure out how to address someone you don't know. It is always appropriate (as a sign of respect) to refer to someone you are newly meeting as *Sir* or *Ma'am.* As soon as it's practical, ask them how they would like to be addressed. If you are an s-type, do not feel obligated to be submissive to anyone/everyone who clams to be a D-type: many women who are new to BDSM believe at first that they have to be submissive to everyone and go out of their way to show how submissive they can be. Don't do this: it can get you tagged either as *low-hanging fruit* or as a *doormat.* Both are easy prey for carnivorous Dom/mes.

When you are being introduced to someone, keep in mind that the D-type or s-type only have authority/responsibility within the context of their own relationship. That is, the D-type can tell HIS or HER s-type what to do, but has no authority to tell YOU what to do. It is outrageously presumptuous for a Dom/me who is **not** in a relationship with an s-type to treat that person *as if* they have some authority over them. Unfortunately, this is a lesson many Dominants seem to have missed when they were studying for their Kink License.

Commanding respect

You probably don't typically think much about whether or not your words and actions are specifically showing respect. You probably have a wide range of behavior you accept from others before you become personally offended. The BDSM culture differs from your every-day world because you're now being exposed to people who have come together over *common interests* as opposed to *common backgrounds*. You're gong to run into some folks with $1 million in their bank accounts and you're gong to run into people deeply in debt. You're going to run into people with advanced degrees and you're going to run into people who never made it out of high school. In this setting, how you respect others will be reflected back in the respect others show to you.

Just because someone is older than you doesn't mean that they have more experience than you. Just because someone who identifies as a 25 year old Master with 10 years experience doesn't mean that he is clueless. In this culture, respect is given to those who are senior in age and those who are senior in experience: to those who are male and to those who are female – regardless of their chosen relationship role. Obvious disrespect and public bashings are not tolerated. Again, how you treat others is noticed and tells those who are watching a lot about the type of person you are.

Now here's a caution concerning respect: Some s-types get so caught up in our culture that they seem to forget that simply as *people*, they deserve the same respect that would naturally be given to a D-type. Some s-types believe as though it's their place to be treated *less than* their Dom/Master; they permit themselves to be treated as though they have less value/worth as human beings. This mindset can lead an s-type to permit themselves to be treated badly and/or permit their own needs to remain unaddressed and unfulfilled. I suspect there are at least two reasons for this:

1. D/s and M/s relationships appear on the surface mostly to be about s-types fulfilling their D-type's desires,
2. The Judeo/Christian Western culture supports female submission to male dominance.

The reality, of course, is that a submissive won't remain in a relationship with a partner who is unable to recognize their core needs as a person. If the sub's desires continue to remain unaddressed, they'll leave to find a partner who is a better fit for them.

When PhoenixRed read through this book, she mentioned that she sees a parallel to this—especially with online subs that behave as though it's the dominant's *job* to give them everything they want and need. She commented that she is frequently astonished to watch as these online subs treat Dominants like civil service workers instead of skilled practitioners of their craft. These Internet subs seem not to understand that it can take many years for a Top to become proficient in SM activities—and that there's a similarly long learning curve involved in understanding how to run a D/s dynamic. The Tops buy the SM toys, go to workshops, and provide just about everything for the relationship. Some of these princess-type subs just want to be doted on and spoiled. Worse, they usually don't stay around long if their attitude toward service and obedience isn't sincere: SAMS (Smart-Assed Masochists), brats and topping-from-the-bottom subs are well represented in the ranks of the newbies.

Similar to the situation about submissives, a bullying Dom/me won't stay around long, either; their behavior fosters wariness among other Dom/mes and creates hostility and tension within a group. Dom/mes don't like to be Dommed by other dominants—of either gender. There is a *submissives network* in most BDSM communities and the word about a bad Dominant spreads like a wildfire. In most cases, the BDSM culture does not support bullying Dom/mes.

Protecting your reputation

The way one personally handles situations makes or breaks one's reputation. There is a fine line between a Dom and a bully, between a Domme and a bitch. In each case, the issue is whether or not the person can handle *authority* with responsibility and grace: the issue is whether they become caught up in the image that they're projecting or whether they are truly projecting their authentic selves.

This is not the book to go into details about building your personal reputation. That's a more advanced book and although I'm considering writing such a work, I haven't fully outlined it yet. That said, consider this:

- We build our lives on the details.
- Decisions select the details that constitute the Path.
- Decisions must be communicated with honesty and clarity.
- The D-type's task: Not only to see the best in the present but also to see what is best in the future.
- Consistent behavior is controlled by *intent*.

So: look inward. Conduct an inventory of your ethical and moral behavior. As I've said: you're now entering a parallel universe where nobody knows you. You can remake yourself.

Or not. It's up to you.

And, sooner or later, you'll find examples of those who are intolerant of others in the community, or you'll find someone who will only befriend those who will fall under their influence. Often, such people will tell you that you (or someone you know) isn't a *real Dom* or isn't *really Leather* or doesn't know how to act like a *real submissive*. Please realize that the person telling you this may be trying to make themselves appear *more than* the person in question by speaking ill of them.

These behaviors drag down our community: so far as the individual goes, is a big red flag. This is personal insecurity leading to public incivility and discourtesy. While many of us preach that there is no *right* or *wrong* way to do BDSM, there absolutely *are* safe and unsafe practices. Similarly, there absolutely *are* respectful and disrespectful behaviors; there absolutely *is* tolerance and intolerance.

Look, folks—we're all just folks: we're all trying to do things that we enjoy. Along the way, we've discovered that there are others out there who—to our surprise and delight—seem also to enjoy similar things. To the vanillas, we're all social outcasts here in the world of taboo sex.

It sure would be nice if us kinksters could be as open minded toward one another as we keep wishing the vanillas would be towards those of us who practice BDSM. It sure would be nice if our fellow kinksters could accept one another regardless of our kinks rather than resorting to pigeonholing and isolating who are a little bit weirder than we think we are. "Oh, he's a *furry*. Shit, can you believe that!" "Oh, he thinks he's so Leather; he doesn't even know what 'Leather' is!" "Look at that guy over there, he's being led around by a collar! He must be pussy-whipped! What a wimp!"

We're involved in BDSM for our own reasons. We're here to have fun as we explore who we are. How dare we judge others who are also here to explore who they are!

Let me introduce you to a different world

How can I explore this world of D/s?
In five words: Explore it slowly and carefully.

But anyway, which form of Dominance and submission? The way it works in world of Gor or the way it works in the world of Daddies and pets or in the world of Masters and slaves?

D/s relationships have different rules/customs; this is a world in which people can explore who they are and how they relate to others. In the words of my good friend Bob Ritchey (Bydarra on Fet), "BDSM is a conversation not a description." That is as true for relationship structures as it is for SM play.

Many people discover BDSM through literature; they read something that gets them going. Please bear in mind that literature is meant to titillate, not to educate. It may sound hot to be locked in a room or a cage while your Dom/me goes off to work for the day, but it is not a healthy practice in real life.

So, the first step is to find out enough to identify what you're interested in.
- Do you have specific fantasies or fetishes you want to fulfill?
- In what role or roles do you see yourself?
- Do you want to *experience* intense physical sensations or *give them*?
- Do you want to *serve* others or to *be served*?

You can pick and choose, mix and match, combine until the cows come home. And, I'm sure that there is a kink somewhere about cows coming home.

This is the world where you can be a dominant masochist (you're running the show, but you like intense physical sensations mixed in with your sex) or a sadistic submissive (you prefer to follow than to lead but you get off on hurting someone a little—or a lot). You can participate actively in BDSM whether or not you know your power dynamic (dominant or submissive) or whether or not you even like the physical SM activities (maybe you just like to watch). You may also play in this pond with or without sexual interaction, for while sex is assumed by many, sex is most certainly **not** assumed by others.

What a surprise! It's a culture…and it will be as challenging to become comfortable here as it would be if you moved abroad. Similarly, you'll adapt more easily to some aspects of our BDSM culture than others. Think about it… while it may not be too hard to adapt to life in London, just imagine trying to adapt to life in a remote African or Tibetan village.

It can be hard to figure out what's going on
In this day and age, people can find out about BDSM from many sources. You can pick and choose to be involved at any level—from reading books to having long talks with a personal mentor whom you met through a local BDSM club. You can spend time on BDSM-specific social networking sites (the most notable being FetLife.com) attend educational presentations at your BDSM club, or you can immerse yourself in the dozens of presentations and demonstrations that are offered at a weekend BDSM conference from coast to coast. You can watch SM play in the privacy of your own home (on BDSM-themed porn sites), at public dungeons, BDSM club parties, and at private parties held in people's homes. As I said, you can choose to be as involved or uninvolved as you would like.

But, without some degree of knowledge and experience, it can be hard to figure out what you're seeing because much of the time, what you think that you're seeing (unless it's a porn show) isn't exactly what's happening. BDSM is not the world of WYSIWYG.

This is a world
Where *what is*
Often isn't what you think it is,
Even if you've been here a while.

It often turns out
That even though
You think that you know something very well,
What you think you know
Turns out to be
Simply not so.

In fact,
This is a world
Where things are not now how they used to
be,
Even before you started,
Because everyone's experience of the way
Things were
And should be
Differs and conflicts and gets
Blended together
Until what is and what was
Becomes only what is or was for you or for me
And seldom
Makes the same kind of sense
For the guy or gal sitting next to you
At a
Munch,
Party,
Or club meeting.

—Robert (Dr. Bob) Rubel

WYSIWYG (**W**hat **Y**ou **S**ee **I**s **W**hat **Y**ou **G**et) is actually a technical term from the world of computer programming that means that what you to see on your computer screen is exactly what will appear if you print it.

Transferred into modern English, this acronym means about the same thing: What you're looking at is actually what is going on. While this is true of most things in the world, it turns out to be much less true in the world of BDSM, whether you're watching an SM scene or speaking with a couple about their relationship.

Let's say a friend has invited you to your first BDSM play party. There, you see a man spanking a woman who is crying and begging, "No, please, stop, I didn't do anything!" you would be fairly safe to assume that you're watching a woman being punished by

her partner and that the public spanking may actually be a case of domestic abuse. Now, you might also be surprised/shocked/offended to see a grown man spanking a grown woman in public, but that's secondary to your conclusion that she was being spanked against her will and that something was VERY wrong.

Unlike in the vanilla world, spankings in the world of BDSM are a normal practice and phrases such as: "No! Stop! That's too hard!" are generally taken to be part of a scene rather than a cry for the Top to stop.

So, what's going on with the couple in this example?

Remember, you're at a BDSM play party. The couple may enjoy *domestic discipline* and you're seeing a discipline scene. The couple may be *spankos* (people who get erotic stimulation from giving and/ or receiving a spanking) and you're watching the usual form of bratty banter that belongs in the scene. In this context, the bottom certainly expects that cries of, "No! Stop! That's too hard!" to be delightfully ignored. The bottom knows to use the words *yellow* and *red* to tell the Top when the sensations are *really* getting too intense.

Bottom line: *the emotions that such a scene brings up in **you** are not likely to be the emotions that the scene is bringing up in those who are participating in it.* It's not WYSIWYG.

Continuing along this line of thought, you can go to a BDSM play party and watch someone being flogged or whipped heavily and hear them cry out in apparent anguish and pain yet nobody around them seems to be paying much attention to their cries. Why is this? It's because what *you* are seeing is not what *they* are getting; they are being pleased by the intense sensations, not hurt in the negative sense.

Don't go through the door with your eyes closed

Can you help me? I'm a slave in search of a Master, where should I look?

Because I present nationally on authority-based relationships, and because for many years I have been a volunteer on the Website allexperts.com in the areas of BDSM and Master/slave relations, I am frequently asked where this person can find a Dom or Master. My typical answers are these:

- Be sure you understand what you are looking for—Dom/mes are concerned with *power exchange* and Masters are concerned with *authority transfer:* these are very different worlds;
- Prepare yourself so that when such a person finds you, you are clearly the answer *to their* search;
- Be sure that others in your community hold this Master (or Dom/me) in high regard;
- Understand why this person is available.

Recently my friend Master Arach (blogging as *TheEroticist.Com*) wrote a blog titled: "I am a slave in search of Master" that addressed this topic beautifully. With his permission it is reprinted here with only minor editorial changes.

"I see so many profiles from young people saying so firmly that they are committed to slavery and looking for a Master, or identify totally as a submissive and are looking for a Dominant. Now for those of us with any experience with online communities, we know that the **vast** majority of these profiles are less than honest. But I want to address some thoughts to those that *are* honest.

"My first question to you is: What does it mean to be someone's *submissive* or *slave*? Well, I could venture a guess. I suppose that you are seeking some level of authority exchange—you want someone to make decisions for you whom you serve in some way. Beyond that, it is a free ball. There Are No Rules.

"Entering into a relationship as a submissive or slave is a complex decision that can affect your entire life. **You** should be able to state whether or not you want it to affect your career, your relationships with your family or friends, your finances, your ability to travel. **You** should be able to say whether or not you must be *out* to all who know you, if you want to display marks from your beatings, the safety of your sexual or SM play, and so forth. There is no reason why you should follow the rules of someone you are just beginning to know, just because they call themselves a Dominant. As rude as it may sound, make them prove it, let them earn your trust, make sure they match you, and the only way that can happen is by knowing what it is **you** want and being able to communicate it.

"The Eroticist"

The world of BDSM is about communication—both verbal and physical

As you gain experience in BDSM, you'll realize that some of the intense sensations you're giving or receiving actually hurt and can be is risky, edgy, or dangerous. (I know, you're thinking: "Oh, my! What a surprise!") To keep the *good pain* (oh fuck oh fuck oh fuck) from turning into *bad pain* (OUCH! STOP THAT!), the person receiving the pain has to know it's coming—**and has to have agreed that they think it is going to be a good idea.** I've put part of the sentence in bold to stress that the bottom has an obligation to *think* and to communicate those thoughts.

Take *rough body play* as an example. In rough body play, the Top strikes the bottom. The strike can be on the upper back or on the fleshy part of the chest or other places that you'll learn over time. The fact that the bottom likes to be struck during a play scene does NOT mean that the same bottom likes to be struck by that same Top without warning when out in a shopping mall. The same actions that can be viewed as SM *play* when done with *consent*, can—without consent—carry the aura of **abuse**.

This is where communication and intent come into play. You have to talk about what you intend to do to someone—and that person has to agree that they think that what you're planning on doing to them is a good idea. This is called *negotiation*. It is considered **highly unethical** for a Top to do something to a bottom in a play scene that has not been pre-negotiated. Reputations can be lost in a moment if a Top does something to a bottom that hadn't been negotiated—even if they've been partners for years. (You might want to read that last sentence a few times. I'm currently observing a case that may well end up in the courts. A Top's non-consensual non-negotiated act in a private play scene terminated a six-year relationship. He performed an act that he absolutely knew was off-limits for his partner—and he ignored her repeated pleas for him to stop. His action caused *serious* harm and her well-documented medical complications have now lasted more than a year. Horrifyingly, the Dom was exceedingly well known and respected in his community and the woman who was hurt is a senior professional in a school district. Neither are dummies. Yes, the police became involved.)

Because it's so important to negotiate *who does what to whom* in BDSM-based relationships, you'll find many relevant topics at weekend BDSM conferences (see Supplement C for a weblink that lists them). But, there's another point here: If you find yourself in a BDSM-based relationship and there's not a lot of talking going on, chances are that the D-type and the s-type are not on the same page. The inability to communicate openly and freely is a leading indicator of relationship troubles that will only be made worse/more intense because of the BDSM component. This is true, because the BDSM component requires both trust and empathy in order to function: communication problems tie directly to trust issues. More trust = more play; broken trust = no play.

Now, communication in the world of BDSM comes in two forms: communicating through words and communicating through SM play, itself. We've just gone over verbal communication; let's now take a look at communication through SM activities.

This next point may be a bit controversial and I have never seen it written out before. I'd like to set the situation up this way: People play for different reasons...

- Some people are playing with the intention of *practicing their skills,*
- Others are playing with the intention of *having their own needs met,*
- Still others are playing with the intention of *connecting with the person with whom they're playing.*

You can pretty well tell the intention of most SM scenes by watching the ending. For those practicing their skills, when the scene is over, it's over. The Top may say: Okay girl x, get dressed; someone else wants to use the St. Andrews Cross—hurry up." Not much connection, and chances are that the bottom was not destined for a trip to subspace.

When you watch players who are playing with the intention of having their own needs met, you may be looking at a sadist who wishes to cause discomfort and pain paired with a masochist who wishes to be *used* by the sadist (for reasons unique to that person). In these situations, the bottom may not much care whether the sadist is connecting emotionally with them, for they are letting their body be used by their sadistic partner, and their own pleasure or enjoyment may not be part of the equation.

As you watch some scenes, though, you'll see an extremely connected pair, as the sadistic Top requires a high degree of connection with the masochistic bottom in order to get his own thrills: he wants to read the *surprise, fear,* and *pain* in their eyes and is an expert in reading a person's physical actions/reactions as a gauge of their mental state. Again, the bottom's pleasure may not be a factor in this play, but it's still a highly connected kind of play.

So where are we? What's the message? The message is that it's not WYSIWYG. You can have people doing the same activities with different intentions obtaining different outcomes. As you learn to appreciate the nuances of scenes you'll begin to think of the SM interactions as a form of very intense communication and (often) bonding.

We've been discussing competent Tops working safely with willing bottoms. But not every Top is competent or safe, and not every bottom is fully willing—some have been bullied or coerced into bottoming. There are some indicators that will help you identify people who are following a different kind of agenda than we've been discussing. Noticing these things will help you to determine who you may wish as your next bottom or Top.

Next time you're at a play party, notice the Top who is doing *showy* things.

- Is this Top personally insecure and playing to the audience, or is what at first appeared to be *showing off* really providing a series of distinct sensations aimed at sending the bottom on a trip to the moon?

- Observe whether the Top is establishing and maintaining physical touch and/or consistent eye contact with the bottom—or barely noticing them. Watch for the connection. Watch for those who are communicating through SM play and befriend them; learn from them.

  Watch for Tops who appear to be disconnected from their bottoms and learn from them, too: learn to discern whether the lack of connection is a valid and negotiated part of the scene (a good Top doing what was negotiated) or whether you're watching an emotionally disconnected scene that is giving little or nothing to the bottom (an emotionally detached Top who is *not* delivering what was negotiated).

Often those new to BDSM agree to try something new in order to gain the experience—rather like earning merit badges in the Scouts. However, in their rush to shed the *newbie* tag they can lose track of the idea that they're supposed to be having fun. They may permit themselves to be played by someone with whom they should not be playing.

Remember: it's okay to say, "No."

Chapter 2
Developing a BDSM-based relationship

It's complicated

When you boil it all down, *living* is comprised of three conceptual categories:

- your relationships with people (the degree and extent of emotional connection and love);
- the structure of those relationships (who is in charge; roles and behaviors with others); and
- your sexual preferences (both in terms of traditional sex and kinky sex).

While I have no way of helping you with the degree and extent of your emotional connections with people, I believe that I can offer you quite a bit of help when it comes to explaining about kinky relationships and kinky sex. Of course, this is the book covering the *relationships* part of the equation.

Personally, I believe that that people who are comfortable to be around know a lot about themselves: they know their own wants and needs. Their personal comfort helps to make others feel comfortable. It follows that the more comfortable you makes others feel, the more appealing you are to people looking for a partner—whether it's for temporary BDSM play or for a possible relationship. In that light, this book is designed to help you learn more about yourself and your own wants and needs.

Before I start in on this chapter, I'd like to say something to those of you who are considering setting up (or who are already involved in) a D-type/s-type relationship structure.

We all have hopes. We all have hopes for our relationships. We all have hopes that our own special partner will turn out to be the spectacular person we love so much. But, as you well know, *hope* doesn't sustain a relationship. Relationships take work, and in my own experience, BDSM relationships are far more complex and require far more work than vanilla relationships. This is particularly true when the D-type in an authority-imbalanced relationship requires their s-type to live within a set of standards that carry consequences for disobedience. Sooner or later each partner is going to be tested: it helps if you account for that reality at the front-end of a relationship.

For those of you in the business world, let me translate that into project-planning language: you need anticipate critical failure points and work them into your plan. In BDSM-based relationships, there are two glaring critical failure points:

- Not every self-professed D-type is worthy of respect, adoration, loyalty, and the gift of an s-type just because they say they are a Dom/me.
- Not every self-professed s-type is going to be perfectly obedient, want to work within the structure the dominant provides, and be inherently worthy of the gift of a D-type simply because they say they are a submissive.

Relationships in this culture are more complicated than you might currently imagine.

About finding a partner— whether short- or long-term

Finding a partner starts with checking references, whether you are a Top or bottom. More can go wrong on a BDSM date than on a vanilla date: the more you know about someone before you go out, the greater your chance that you'll have a stellar experience.

Checking references

Some of us in the BDSM world require a personal reference as the number-one basic requirement even for an e-mail exchange. Others of us feel that we can't have too many friends and welcome anyone who wants to contact us. While e-mail exchanges with someone unknown to you doesn't pose much of an issue other than taking up your time, should the e-mails and IMs start to lead to thoughts of actually *meeting*, most of us would urge you to find out something more about this person—male or female, Top or bottom.

Now... if someone *can't* provide references to someone that you actually know, that may be because they don't participate in the public BDSM community. That's not necessarily a red flag, but it would certainly signal you to add another layer of caution. After all, if they don't participate in the public scene, where did they get their SM skills training? It's going to be a judgment call whether or not you meet this person—and where you meet them.

On the other side of this coin, I would argue that if someone *won't* provide references to someone that you actually know—if you keep asking for references and they keep dodging the question—it's a serious issue. After all, you'd think that anyone trustworthy living close enough to you to physically meet you must know someone who can vouch for them.

So—yes, you're going to want to ask for and check references. But, as with many things in life, this can be more easily said than done. In the first place, you (yourself) have to be well enough established in your BDSM community even to know *whom* you can ask about another person. That is, until you actually know someone a little bit, you can't trust their answer whether they tell you that person-X would be a good or bad play partner for you. The person you ask may not like the person you're asking about for non-BDSM reasons and give you a thumbs-down, or the person you're asking may be a total pain slut, not know that you're a really light player, and give you a thumbs up. Wrong in either case, right?

Let me lighten this up, some. If you have been in the community long enough to have mutual friends, then by all means, ask away. That's a pretty normal part of social interaction. You can say: "Hey, I'm going out with Dave next week, you know him, right? Good guy?"

On the other hand, trying to get a reference from a stranger about another stranger is not going to make quite as much sense. While it makes sense to try to assess a possible play partner's reputation and obtain some references, there are some limitations in this area that some folks seem to overlook.

Speak with someone who knows the person you're interested in...

Listen for what you are NOT being told, as well as what you are being told. Listen for unusual phrasing: "Oh, gosh, sure I know *lovelybod (or bigstud)*. Oh, I don't think it's appropriate for me to say anything about her/him—that would sound too much like gossip, you know what I mean?"

Because our community relies so heavily upon personal endorsements, it's *extremely important* that you couldn't get one for *lovelybod/ bigstud*. Your follow-up question might be: "Oh, can you give me the name of anyone who might know her/him?"

If your source now says something like: "Oh, gosh, that would really be hard. I just don't know...." you know that you've just unfurled a red flag. Be *very* cautious.

It's not enough to hear, "So-and-so is a bitch" or "I'd be careful of him, if I were you." You need to ask WHY this person is saying that. The potential problem with taking someone's word at face value is that our community seems to have something of a *lemming response* when saying that someone is bad or icky; some who repeat the gossip can't exactly explain why they're warning you off. And the *why* often turns out to be because someone else said they were bad or icky. And if you track *that* person down, they'll tell you that they're not quite sure, but that *everybody* knows that the person in question is not someone you'd want to know.

Often, when you get information about someone, you're not dealing with first-hand knowledge. Frequently, you're not even dealing with second-hand knowledge. You're being fed a line of local myth or lore. The longer people are in a community, the more likely it is that some myth or lore has built up around them. It's their *reputation*. Which brings me back to something I said back in the Introduction: in this community, you live and die by your word. In this community, your words demonstrate your honor and your actions demonstrate your ethics. You are on stage every time you show up to a BDSM club meeting or play party. And, it's a small stage. Once you become active in our world, you'll be amazed how quickly everyone knows someone who knows someone who knows you—or at least knows *of* you and has formed some kind of uninformed opinion of you.

Message: you're going to want to know a bit about the person you're approaching for a reference to the third party:
- How long have they been involved with BDSM?
- How long have they been members of what organizations?
- Are they evaluating this person for you as a potential SM play partner or as a possible date?

Then, you'll want to ask this person about how well they know this other person:
- How long have they known this person? What's the back-story; how did they meet them? Do they know this person outside of the BDSM community?
- What is their overall impression of this person? Are they a team player or do they sort-of keep to themselves?
- Have they seen this person play? Ask them to tell you about it. Would they play with this person or recommend that others play with them? Why or why not?
- What is this person's strength, skill, personality, reputation...?
- Do they have any concerns about this person's play style that you should be aware of?

This list is not meant to lead to an inquisition; these are the questions to which you're seeking answers from a casual conversation. "That guy over there, BigGuy, he seems like a nice guy, do you happen to know him… ? Interesting play style, do you know anyone whose played with him?"

You get the idea…

If at all possible, attend an event and watch the person you're interested in. See how they fit in with your community; watch how they play, either as a Top or bottom.

I made a strident point in the first book in this series that I'll repeat here: When you get to the point that you want to play with someone, please play with this person in public, FIRST. Don't agree to a private scene until you feel comfortable and you've established a comfortable level of trust. There are bat-shit-crazy people of either gender out there, and while the stereotype is that men are the transgressors, I know of cases where crazy ladies have created unbelievable drama within a community.

Oh, and you may want to have someone you trust observe that first scene. Sometimes chaperones are a good thing. I'm just sayin'…

What does a *good partner* look like?
Our community contains mostly bright, dynamic, and interesting people. It also contains some really average people. And, too, it contains some icky people. Self-delusion being what it is, they probably won't think that they're presenting problems within the community, but others do. In an effort to start you out on the right foot, here are some positive characteristics to look for in a potential partner. By the way, these are the behaviors *others are looking for when they consider YOU.*

- They are open and giving and generally see the best in people. They use a *cooperative* model and like to work with others for mutual benefit. They are slow to say anything negative about others and do not pass on second-hand information. They do not think in terms of *them and us* but are inclusive by nature. They think of themselves as part of a community rather than a person central to the community. Their behavior does not draw attention.

- If they are a D-type, they fit in well with other dominants; if they are an s-type, they fit in well with other submissives. They will not be drawn into cliques, controversy, or drama. They appreciate a wide range of viewpoints and try to understand how the views and opinions of others can benefit their own learning (or benefit the two of you, if you're in a relationship with them). They consider the views of others to be as valuable as their own views.

- They seek counsel from Elders—those who have been in the scene a long time and are generally recognized as wise and trustworthy—because they realize how enriching those people's experiences can be for those that will listen with an open heart.

- As a team player, they are careful to credit others where credit is due. As with all undertakings, they take time to study and to learn about the depth and breadth of the BDSM world.

- When they find that a decision is opposed, they stop and consider the context of the opposition: if the issue concerns a difference of opinion, they accept it as that; if the issue concerns matters of fact or conclusions seemingly based on facts, they will go back and check what they know of the facts and the assumptions upon which they are built. In negotiations, they are committed to win-win solutions.

- They seem to have lots of friends who also seem to last a long time. You sometimes worry that they put the needs of others before their own needs. If they wanted to give a party, their first thought could be "Gosh, where can I find a place big enough?"

- They love being with you and support your growth and development. They encourage you to socialize with other club members and to attend all the kink-related events that you can. They speak lovingly (or at least not negatively) about others they have loved in the past.

- They abhor gossip and have a firm policy of repeating only experiences about which they have first-hand knowledge. They realize that everyone has bad-hair days.

- They are well thought of by the senior members of the club and by those with whom whey work.

The message, here, is that those who are generally well-adjusted and successful make good partners and those who have personality challenges at work, with friends, and within their own families will probably be a challenge for anyone close to them.

But... how do you *know* they're okay?

A bit of a reality check, here: just as you can find male dominants that are pretenders (wannabe's or weekend-warriors), users, abusers, and financial predators, you can also find female submissives that are manipulative, crafty, and needy. You can find women with a plan in the world of BDSM: they label themselves *submissive* to attract male dominants that will take care of them. Often, these are women who have mastered the arts of deception, misrepresentation, and manipulation in order to get what they want.

These women are not really submissives at all; they know a great deal about the BDSM way of life and have learned how to work the BDSM system to infiltrate the life of someone they feel they may be able to manipulate. Some simply want to be taken care of; others have a more sinister purpose. Because they are experienced, they can be very hard to identify. I personally watched a *submissive* fleece three men before I could bring myself to recognize her for the financial predator that she was. She was lithe, gorgeous, a very heavy bottom (could take a LOT of pain), and very well trained in formal Leather protocols. She turned heads. She had good stories and I was too trusting.

PhoenixRed, who hosts a weekly online chat room for people new to BDSM, said that she, too, has had problems with female dominants who seem only to want to be spoiled and pampered. She has noticed that these women want gifts and tributes without offering the man any of the *activities* for which they are supposedly paying. She says that many of these women prefer heavy humiliation and financial domination (fetishes, by the way), to physical SM activities. Some of these women behave this way because of some real or perceived mistreatment by men in their past relationships. These women are just as bad as dominant male sexual predators. They can just as easily ruin the life of someone who is too trusting.

As you become further involved with another person, you'll want to know more about them. After all, a short-term fling is very different from moving in together. Here are some relationship questions to consider asking a prospective partner – regardless of your role or their role. (You'll have to reword these questions so they sound like you, of course – and also develop other questions to fit your particular circumstances).

- How do your relationships tend to start? How long to they tend to last? And are there common reasons past relationships have ended? (You're looking for patterns, here.)
- Are you employed? In general terms, what is your financial picture? Income, assets, obligations… If this is a Dom interviewing for a submissive/slave, you'll want to be clear about which obligations, if any, will transfer to you. If you're the submissive and are in a better financial condition than the Dom, you'll want to be clear about how much say you'll continue to have about your own income/assets.
- What family obligations do you have? Do you have children or grandchildren? Do you have an aging parent that's gong to need help?
- Do you have any sexually transmitted infections? If not now, have you had any in the past?
- Do you have any chronic or acute medical or psychological conditions?
- Who do you know that I also know? (You'll want to check their social network profiles—do they seem to have a rich social profile? How about their BDSM history/profile on FetLife? Ours is a pretty small community. If you can't get a reference, proceed with extreme caution.)
- Do you describe yourself as an introvert or extrovert? (Attend your local kink meeting with your potential partner. How do they behave? Are they welcomed like a person of high value, or like some gruesome plague? Does this person appear to be surrounded by a closed circle of friends (a clique?), or does this person mix with the general assembly? In fact, what

conclusions can you draw about this person by the others with whom they meet?)

Establishing the right *fit* with a partner

As you're exploring this world of BDSM, as you're meeting potential (possibly long-term) partners, consider whether you like the person because he/she *feeds your kink* or because he/she *matches your core values, wants, and needs.*

A tip (courtesy of my partner, Jen): Write out a list of your ten top *wants* in a partner. As you're searching, find someone who can fill the top eight rather than the bottom eight. If you don't, you risk finding that you can't maintain the relationship long-term because your two most critical needs remain unmet. Your partner will turn into an annoyance.

A tip (courtesy of me being seriously older than you and having Asperger Syndrome): When you're visiting your potential partner's house/apartment, pay attention. Do you just *love* the way they decorate and how well they maintain their personal space? You'll have to trust me on this: it's the little things about a person (such as their personal tastes and habits) that often foretells a comfortable or uncomfortable future relationship. Some people (myself, as an Aspie) have very firm attitudes about *how things should look and be arranged*. It can be hard (or impossible) for a neuro-typical to understand what it can do to a relationship when one person prefers the furniture to be of X style rather than of Z style, or when the candles are placed on the mantle in X fashion rather than Y fashion. As the saying goes: *The Devil's in the details.*

Aligning your relationship
Finding good "partner material" can be a huge ordeal; I get it. However, finding someone who generally meets your needs leaves you two more step to go: First, you'll want to be sure that you both agree upon the *purpose* for being a couple, and second, you'll want to be certain that your particular kinks are aligned. I've prepared some points for you to consider.

Here are some questions aimed at getting your relationship *intent* straight. These are questions to help you think about the *purpose* and *focus* of a relationship.

- Are you seeking a power-imbalanced relationship or a love-based relationship—or some combination of those elements? That is, if this is an s-type looking for a D-type, is it to be primarily a love-based or service-based relationship?

- Are you seeking a D/s or M/s relationship structure (power exchange or authority transfer)? Said differently, are you a submissive seeking a Dom or a slave seeking a Master? (And, what do these roles *mean* to each of you???)

- If you are *not* seeking an authority-imbalanced relationship, then are you primarily interested in an authority-equal relationship centered around SM play? In that case, are you a bottom seeking a Top or a Top seeking a bottom?

- Are each of you looking for play partners? For a short-term relationship? For long-term commitment?

- Have you dealt with past trauma/abuse issues? Have you been through therapy to resolve those issues? *Do you know the kind of baggage you are bringing into the relationship?*

- Are you the best relationship partner that you think you can be right now? If not, in what areas should you begin working on yourself?

- Have you discussed monogamy, serial polyamory, multiple polyamory with or without sex, and swinging? Is each of you clear about your roles/responsibilities for whichever of these activities or structures you intend to pursue?

- If you're a Dom/Master, are you looking for a multi-person structure (Master and multiple slaves)? If you're a slave/submissive, are you entering an established structure as a beta slave reporting to the established Alpha? If you're entering an established multi-person family, are you expected to be sexually intimate with the others? If you're entering a relationship as a slave, can you be loaned out or actually given away?

Aligning your kinks

- Is your life to be centered on sadomasochism (SM) or something else?
- What aspects of the scene appeal to each of you (SM play, role play, psychological play)?
- If SM, what flavor? Same as your partner?
  - How will you handle it if you don't really like to participate in your partner's kink? (My current partner likes to stick needles in male bottoms: that's not my thing.)
  - How will you handle it if your partner needs more than you can offer?
  - Are you interested in exploring edgy taboos? Issue: what is *edgy* to one person may be pretty tame to someone else.
- What kind of porn do you like to watch together? Is the bottom being pampered with sensations or screaming in agony as she's being whipped with nettles? Is the bottom elaborately bound and suspended or is she being forced to orgasm with vibrators? The key question: Do your sadistic and masochistic preferences match?
- If you're an s-type and you're looking for a sadistic D-type, you probably want to explore the reasons why this person likes giving pain. You need to be able to distinguish between a BDSM Dom/me and an abuser. Some people are really Class III sadists (discussed earlier) who pretend to be BDSM Dom/mes as they are searching for easy prey. They are abusers who use their victims as physical and/or emotional punching bags and give physical/mental pain because they are cruel. They prey on s-types that have low self-esteem and who think they deserve no better.

It is important to know answers to these and similar questions before getting too far into a relationship, as the answers can save you a lot of heartache down the road—whether the *you* in this sentence is a D- or s-type.

Connecting emotionally with your partner

In a general way, you can divide sexual play into two categories: sex with connection and sex without connection.

Sex without connection, while often a lot of fun, is not particularly rewarding for many people. While **one** participant may be having a great time, the other participant often is left feeling unsatisfied or unfulfilled. For unconnected sex, it doesn't particularly matter *who* your partner is; you are focused on your own sexual needs and release.

Sex *with* connection is what vanillas dream of: this is love-based sex where each partner cares tremendously about the others' pleasure and is fully engaged in both the giving and receiving of pleasure. Sex with connection can go on for hours and hours. Sex with can expand into a form of bonding that has each partner awakening in the morning and looking forward to that night's adventure—years into the relationship, well after the *new relationship energy* has worn off.

As you become more advanced in your SM techniques, you will

A Private Note that is Relevant
Name withheld; used with permission.

I've been to a couple of your presentations and I do love them. The first one I saw was on impact play at (event name) and you used a demo bottom that was not your partner. Until I saw your demo I was starting to doubt that impact play was for me. I'd been to parties and had seen a lot of people beating on folks for the action of doing it—which just felt flat.

Your demo was the first time I saw connection in the process. You paid so much attention to her, touching her—and in between sensations you listened to her ... damn it was sexy to watch! I left that demo saying "That's what I'm talking about!" ... oh and a little wet from arousal as well. ;) So thank you for helping me realize that I not only like impact play, but I require connection and intimacy in the process. ;)

learn how to connect intentionally with your play partner, whether or not that person is in a relationship with you. The difference between sex/BDSM play with and without connection is huge.

The way sex is practiced in America (even the way it is portrayed in most straight porn movies and popular romance novels), both partners have a pretty equal say about what is going on. The girl is looking forward to the sexual encounter as much as the guy; she tears his clothes off about as fast as he tears her clothes off. In mainstream porn, there are certain positions that we have come to expect: she gives him a blow job; he eats her out; he takes her through about five standard anal and vaginal penetration positions by plunging in and out (evidently oblivious to any skilled use of his cock, something I've always found astonishing) and they have orgasms. Well, the guy has an orgasm that is impossible to disguise and the girl is probably faking it. It's hard to find porn flicks that show a man who is reading the girl's reactions and bringing her along on the ride. It's also hard to find porn films showing a guy that is skilled at fucking: those that know what they're dong immediately stand out.

At best, most of us start our sex lives using the techniques we observed in vanilla porn movies: after all—these guys are getting paid to do *it* so this *must* be the right way, right? And, there aren't courses to take. When relationships are new, new relationship energy is enough to keep the sex hot and interesting for a while. However, many couples find that over time, their intense sexual flame burns lower and lower and neither partner quite knows how to recapture what they remember so vividly as peak sexual experiences. The magic spark that came to them mysteriously has somehow left them mysteriously. Western sexual culture does not help them to decode the sexual mystery. That's where BDSM can help.

Many of the rules/standards/expectations that you will learn as you delve further into BDSM can help you to pick a good partner, the BDSM culture can show you paths and options you didn't know existed, and the BDSM culture can safely expose you to skills and sensations that can capture your imagination and change your life.

Emotional safety

Although emotional safety is seldom mentioned in BDSM books—even in books specifically explaining safety in SM play—it is an important topic both for those new to BDSM and for established couples.

The term *emotional safety* refers to how emotionally comfortable we are in a relationship. When we feel emotionally safe, we can speak freely and openly; when we feel emotionally unsafe, we are mentally on-guard when we speak.

As a general rule, people choose friends with whom they can speak freely—with whom they feel emotionally safe. All of us subconsciously monitor our emotional safety whenever we are with another person. Our understanding of emotional safety begins when we take the time and trouble to understand what we need and want from our relationships with others and how we value ourselves. I've summarized some aspects of *emotional safety in order* to give you a sense of this huge topic.

- **Feeling respected:** Do you support your partner's wants and needs? Do you keep their needs forefront in your thoughts and actions?
- **Feeling heard:** Do you use *active listening* with your partner? How do you let your partner know that you are paying attention to them? Does your partner complain that you ignore, tune out, or speak condescendingly to them? (Active listening: before replying, you repeat the essence of what someone said to confirm that you responding to the correct message.)
- **Feeling understood:** Do you make time to ensure that you know what's going on with your partner and to change your own behavior to honor your partner's needs? Has your partner expressed frustration that you are just not *getting* them or that you are twisting their words to produce meanings different than they intended?
- **Feeling validated:** Do your actions validate your partner? That is, even if you don't agree with your partner, do you at least acknowledge what your partner has said or is feeling? Do you agree to disagree?

- **Showing empathy:** Do you know how to express empathy toward your partner in the *love language* that they understand? NOTE: a lack of empathy in a relationship probably means that you're out of sync with their emotions. The partner experiencing a lack of empathy can experience a great deal of sadness or anger. Has your partner ever expressed a sentiment such as, "You don't care how I feel."
- **Feeling loved:** Do you have some way to calibrate how much you feel loved by your partner and how much your partner feels your love? This can be a challenge, but it should generate some good discussions. This *feeling loved* topic is the rough barometer for the other five states. People who report low levels of *feeling loved by the other* typically have low emotional responses in the other aspects. (Although this category is most relevant to people beginning or involved in a relationship, it still applies to casual SM play. Rather than *feeling loved*, just substitute *feeling liked* or *made to feel important*.)

Note #1: If you're not familiar with discussions about *love languages*, you might wish to do some Internet research. You also may wish to research *processing modalities* to be sure that you know how to recognize whether the person takes in information best through sight, sound, touch, smell, or taste. This is an important area: you'll need to know *how* the person with whom you're speaking wishes you to explain things to them. For example, do they want you to explain things verbally (they process orally) or do they want you to give them something to read (they process visually)? For an in-depth discussion of this and many other communication topics, see my book: *Master/ slave Relations: Communication 401—the advanced course.*

Note #2: Some of us have different brain wiring than *normal* people (neuro-typicals). Those of us on the Autism Spectrum Disorder scale (which is where *Aspies* like me live) may have trouble with many/ most topics on this list: they'll likely have the *most* trouble connecting empathetically with others. For us, vanilla relationships can be stressful and intense BDSM-based relationships can prove extraordinarily challenging. See Supplement B for suggested reading if you think that you or your partner has Asperger Syndrome—now called *high-functioning Autism.*

Establishing safewords for emotional hurt

Disturbances in one partner's feelings of emotional stability/safety can threaten the relationship as a whole. When one partner is upset at the other, they're not going to be in the mood for sex or SM play. However, unless you have an established protocol that enables one partner to signal emotional distress to the other, one partner may not realize/understand that the other is upset. So, let me speak about protocols for emotional safewords for a few paragraphs.

Repeated emotional hurts lead to verbal abuse just as much as repeated physical hurts lead to physical abuse. In relationships where one or both of you are using a scene-name, you might consider using your given name as the emotional safeword. That is, if you're going by *cici* as your scene name and your legal name is Cecelia or Nancy or Tabatha (making names up, here), then when your partner uses your legal name rather than your scene name, you are being told that you have just hurt your partner's feelings and they wish to speak about it.

Similarly, if you are the s-type and you're used to calling your D-type *Sir* (or *Ma'am* or *Master/Mistress*) I'm proposing that the two of you establish a protocol that permits you to use his/her legal name in order to communicate that they hurt your feelings. When used, this emotional safeword requires the D-type to come out of whatever headspace they're in and pay full attention to you right now to discuss/disarm the situation. Please bear in mind that unattended emotional hurts can represent a breach of trust. Repeated breaches of trust will doom a relationship. That's another promise, unfortunately.

Here is an example from my personal experiences.

During an emotional exchange, "Master, that's not what I understood you to say!" impacts me very differently than, "Bob, that's not what I understood you to say!" I hear the first version (spoken in our standard speech protocols) to be expressing some (probably minor) confusion that we now need to sort out. However, I hear the second version, expressed in the speech protocol signaling emotional upset, to be expressing quite a few things:

- First, using my actual name—Bob—means that I need to *pay attention.*
- Second, I have either given an unclear message or my partner deciphered it differently than I intended it and this communication gap has just been revealed.
- Third, this perceived communication gap between words and intention has upset my partner emotionally.
- Fourth, I have to take some kind of immediate action to prevent this verbal exchange from escalating.

There is another instance where using one's legal name can be helpful: it can signal an emergency: "Bob, something's not right, here!" gets my attention much more effectively than: "Master, something's not right, here!" In my world, these sentences are *very* different and would elicit *very* different responses from me. In the first instance, I'm up, out of my chair, and alarmed; in the second instance I might look up casually and ask, "Mmmm?" (Note: for eight years I lived in a high-protocol Master/slave relationship; my slave followed certain speech and behavior protocols in private as well as in public.)

Issues to consider as a couple

Communication and trust
BDSM relationships are about trust—and *trust* is built upon honest and transparent communication. You must trust someone in order to give them control over your body. You must trust that if you say *red* they will stop, that they will honor your ultimate control over the scene. You gift them with yourself, but you know that they won't do whatever they are going to do to you without your consent and willingness. It is an amazing gift to place your trust in another person to be responsible for whatever happens to you. Since trust is built as much on communication as it is on consistent, reliable action, successful BDSM relationships involve much more communication than is found in most vanilla relationships.

For the Top: When playing, you need to be able to trust that they will do as they say: you need to trust that as you are learning your skills, your bottom will honestly tell you when the sensations are getting too strong. Unfortunately, you are likely to find bottoms who will take more pain than they really wish because they want to be thought of as a *real submissive* (or some such). They won't *color out* of a scene if they can possibly avoid it.

The point is, in the same way that a bottom must trust that the Top will respect safewords, the Top must trust that the bottom will actually *use* safewords. I know someone who, as a newbie bottom, simply would not use a safeword—*red* or anything else. As it happens, this new bottom was a Domme who had put herself into service to another Dom in order to learn about BDSM. To cure her of her stubbornness, her mentor turned her over to a locally well-known and extremely trustworthy whip master with instructions to make her color out. One strike of his single-tail whip and she screamed *RED!* and ran out of the room clutching her clothing. She promised to use colors in future play. She was my Owner for ten years (during eight of which I lived with the slave she had given me.)

Loving someone vs. being in love with someone

Recently, at the *Leather Reign* conference in Seattle, Washington, Sir Dragon Z commented that, "While *being in love* with someone is an emotional state, *loving someone* is an action." You love your brother or sister; you are not *in love* with your brother or sister. You love your dog or cat; you are not *in love* with your dog or cat. One

Safety Tip

If you want your safeword to work, you will have to practice using it

is not better than the other, but the distinction is important in BDSM where complex relationships are the norm. In this culture, quite a bit of heartache can result from making assumptions about the meaning of words or terms. In BDSM, many words and terms carry new and subtle meanings that never would have occurred to you in your vanilla life.

BDSM relationships differ sharply from vanilla relationships in that romantic/intimate love (being *in love*) is not necessarily required to have a successful relationship. If you're seeking a romantic relationship, you'll want to discuss that along with your other negotiations. Not everyone wants their BDSM partner to be their life-partner or spouse.

At the risk of triggering an avalanche of controversy, I assert that relationship friction often occurs because the dominant partner loves the slave, while the slave is *in love* with the dominant partner. I'd further assert that this distinction is more likely to occur in M/s than in D/s pairings. I believe this is true, because most heterosexual D/s relationships evolve as people are still fairly new to BDSM—a period when both partners are still susceptible to the strong mutual emotional draw of erotic love. Translation: they're transitioning into BDSM from a boyfriend/girlfriend raging-hormones model. People practically never start out in BDSM and go directly to a Master/slave structure. That's something like moving from Los Angeles to Beijing. Nothing wrong with either city; just foreign. Very foreign. You'd want to do a lot of background research before taking that trip.

The Master/slave dynamic can be extraordinarily complex and unlike any relationship structure with which you are familiar—including D/s structures. To learn more, I refer you (again) to my four-volume set on Master/slave relations (start with: *Master/slave Relations: Handbook of Theory and Practice*).

Falling into lust before you fall into logic
If you're new to BDSM—particularly if you have not yet played with anyone—let me offer you a few observations. You're not likely to believe me or act on this information, but let me at least alert you to some common experiences from those of us who have gone before.

First some notes to bottoms. If you have the good fortune to have a play date with an experienced Top, **and** this Top is honest and negotiates without pressuring you about the depth and breadth of the offered play **and** is true to their world and does with you only what they said they would do, **and** is able to make you fly (put you into subspace), you are VERY likely to bond with this person and (often) fall in love on the spot.

After all, you will tell yourself, this must be Some Magical Guy to be able to give you this kind of (what you believe to be) once-in-a-lifetime experience. If this man can do this to you and barely know you, all your emotions will pull you to him without asking a lot of questions. You will think the two of you connected on a *soul level* in order to have achieved this experience. While this may be so, it's far more likely that you have had the great good fortune to find a truly skilled Top to play with you. Although you'll not want to hear it or admit it, this experience is repeatable with another skilled Top.

It is not uncommon for a bottom to fall head-over-heels in love with the person who first played with them (in the BDSM sense). Your first experiences of SM play are likely to bring you to the magic door into a new world. As I say repeatedly, for many of us, it's a one-way door. Once you're in, you're in. Your life will change. Your friends will change. You will either have to begin to lead a quasi-secret life or your relationships with family members will change. Few of us ever want to return to the World of vanillas; that world is just too, well—vanilla.

However, if you have the (more common) experience to have a play-date with someone who has been in the BDSM community for only a few years (or someone who has not invested very much time and effort into learning the social, psychological, and physical skills that one needs to be a competent and safe partner), you may end up with a less-than-stellar experience. Perhaps like your early experiences with traditional sex. Your date may have pushed your boundaries and done a little here and a little there that you wished he hadn't and you'd told him you didn't like/want. Or, your date may have renegotiated with you during the play. That is, you're in the middle of a scene and he asks you (again?) if he can do X and *because you've been having an interesting time,* or *because you're tired of saying "no,"* or *because you're not truly thinking clearly and you're naked,* you say "yes." That may be a *yes* that you later regret, even as you blame yourself for letting him do it. That is, you blame yourself rather than recognize that the person playing with you was unethical to have continued the negotiation process past the start of the scene.

But, if your date gave you a good ride, you may put your questions and concerns away for a while, because the guy/gal is clearly skilled and you weren't hurt. Anyway, you don't yet have enough experience to be able to compare the scene you just experienced with any other scene, so… who knows?

Silver Box experiences

In *Ties that Bind*, Guy Baldwin explains that when a body is skillfully stressed physically (through SM techniques) and/or mentally (through power-exchange techniques) you can produce what he calls an *ecstatic transformation*. Personally, I've come to refer to those as *silver box* experiences; they're so spectacular that you take the memory and put it in an imaginary *silver box* to protect it and to use it to calibrate similar subsequent experiences.

People often start out in a sexually charged BDSM relationship and they want more, more, more of *it* and of one another. That's totally understandable and I've been there. They find that they're now living together and, for a while (perhaps for a long while) the *it* that they're doing together binds them together. But, as the months and years roll on, there are the beginnings of upsets. While the two people are more-or-less on the same page, something is a little *off*. Although they are both speaking the same language, they're not quite speaking the same language, if you know what I mean. I've been there, too. Let me now take a different path and offer those of you starting out a model you may wish to consider as you explore this world.

Men are from Mars…

I've done a fair amount of research and writing about male and female teaching and learning styles, and I've drawn some conclusions that I'd like to share with you. However, I'm telling you up-front that these are my personal *opinions* rather than research-based facts.

My general conclusions are based on the often-noted observations that (particularly in past decades) men tended to be brought up to be competitive problem solvers while most women tended to be brought up to be team players and nurturers. Obviously, there is a lot of crossover learning that people go through, and there are countless competitive female problem solvers and countless male team players and nurturers. Generalizations are always sloppy.

Actually, this makes sense in the context of male/female socialization in the U.S. Consider this and extrapolate: women tend to be brought up to be social and sociable—when out in a group, they often go to the bathroom together. Men, on the other hand, are often brought up to be lone-ranger problem-solvers who play with *things* rather than *people*. When you now consider authority-based relationships in the context of cultural socialization, some interesting patterns emerge:

- Doms seem to put the majority of their focus on how his slave can serve *him* by doing things that save him time or money—or simply please *him*;
- Dommes seem to put the majority of their focus on how *she* can nurture and grow her slave to think more globally and act more responsibly for the benefit of the *relationship*.

Just a thought.

Chapter 3
Finding a Partner

So, let's consider that you are *exploring* a BDSM relationship. You're toying with the idea. But, you've run into a problem. You're having a hard time finding someone that you feel would make a good match for you. I have two thoughts about that: first, stop thinking about finding a partner and think about finding someone with whom you'll have a good time; second, build your skills and broaden your own desirability.

Hmmmmm. Not what you'd expected to find in this book.

Enjoy the process of going out on a date: not every date is with partner material; put *finding a partner* on a back burner for a while. By taking some of the pressure off your dates you open yourself to new experiences. You're putting yourself *out there* where opportunity can happen. I've touched on this idea before. You sure as hell aren't going to find a partner by staying home. *Luck* is *preparation* meeting *opportunity.* Let me spend some time now on the *preparation* part of that equation.

How good are you at assessing yourself? Have you made *introspection* and *self-awareness* part of your life? Do you have the circle of friends that you'd really like to have? Are you in a job/career that you like and that likes you? In your vanilla life, were you attracting the kind of dates you wanted?

If yes, skip this section; if no, read on...

If you're still with me, consider seriously examining yourself. This examination is *for yourself* and not for some possible future partner. You'll have to make a list that is personally relevant, but for starters...

- How's your English—both oral and written? Would you be at home in a graduate-school discussion of some topic, or would you draw attention to yourself? How broad is your vocabulary? Can you pick up a copy of *Scientific American* or *The Economist* and understand what's written? Can you tell stories that captivate your listeners?
- How are your table manners? Know how to pick up a fork? Know how to pat (not *wipe*) *your* mouth with a napkin? Know not to open that napkin more than half way? Know where to place the napkin when you arise from table and are going to be returning versus where you place it if you've finished your meal and are getting up to leave?
- When you enter a room, do you take a moment to check it out? Do you immediately recognize whether or not the room's owner is *highly visual*? Are you able to make distinctions about the owner's social class and personal tastes from the room decorations? Why do this? So you can establish rapport during conversations.
- When you speak, is your voice gentle and pleasing? Do you have a nasal tonality? Have a regional dialect?
- If you hear something spoken, can you identify/isolate key issues and repeat them with accuracy?
- How's your wardrobe? Do you dress fashionably or are you fashion challenged?
- How *flexible* are you, psychologically—can you adapt quickly to changing circumstances, or do you *freeze in the headlights?* (I don't mean *crises*, I mean long-wave life changes. Job retraining, for example.)
- How are you at *conversational magic?* Do you know enough about social intercourse not to speak only about *yourself?* Can you enthrall a potential date for hours by asking leading questions? How broadly can you speak about current events?
- When you are out in public, how closely do you notice people? Do you notice their gestures, their expressions, their mannerisms? For Tops: to play successfully with a bottom, you'll need to be an extremely keen observer. For bottoms: to serve a Dom you'll need to be an extremely keen observer.
- How good are you at problem solving? Ever read any books about it? Same for *branch thinking* vs. *linear thinking*. Can you

think outside of the box (as the saying goes) when solving problems?

- Do you watch TV? Consider limiting your viewing time and read more books. Read widely and learn to discuss what you read. Consider joining a book club. Consider joining Toastmasters. Learn to prepare two and three course meals for yourself. It's a skill you may need later. Dine formally when alone. That way, your good table manners and your ability to put on a beautiful dinner become second nature. No, I have not changed viewpoints; I'm still addressing D-types as much as s-types. This is all about building up the little personal habits—the muscle memory—to master someone else or to serve someone else.

- Are you an expert in some form of BDSM play? Okay, so master another form of BDSM play. And who, if I may be so bold, agrees with you that you ARE a master at some form of BDSM? Does your local kink group ask you to do presentations?

- Do you have a spiritual core? How does your spirituality influence/affect/alter your life?

- Do you have good anger management? Are you carrying difficult *baggage* from your childhood or prior marriage? Have you considered seeing a therapist? Too expensive? Just how costly is it for you NOT to deal with your baggage?

- Learn to interrupt what you are doing, start something else, then come back to what you were doing. Why? Because if you should you ever find yourself *owning* another person, you will need to be sensitive to how you manage that person's time. You'll benefit from knowing how it feels to be interrupted in the middle of a task that you are completing from a list of perhaps a dozen other tasks that all must be completed.

- Learn to do things *completely* and *perfectly*. After all, you are about to enter into an authority-imbalanced relationship where there is *accountability* and *consequences*. That means that either you are going to require this of your partner or your partner is going to require this of you. Either way, you might as well start down this path now: this isn't Kansas anymore, Dorothy. This is a parallel universe in which many people seize this as an opportunity to get their relationships *right* this time. As a D-type, you'll need to be able to lead by example. If you are doing dinner dishes, don't leave the kitchen until all the counters are cleaned and the sinks have been scoured. Hint: Make notes about how you do things— such as dishes and cleaning the kitchen. These notes may well end up as part of your instructions to your s-type OR—if you're the s-type—these notes may become the written proof that you understand how to write protocols.

I'll stop. I could go on, and so could you. This is really a small part of what you are going to have to put yourself through to reinvent yourself in the image you think your partner-to-be would be seeking.

As a D-type—or as an s-type…

Perhaps the greatest incentive to expand skills and experiences is that the new you will likely attract a more versatile partner.

—Robert (Dr. Bob) Rubel

Once you have started mingling with like-minded people, the next hurdle concerns *making an appropriate connection that demonstrates that you are prepared for a relationship.* I would certainly notice it if an s-type came up to me with a card of introduction that *gave just the right amount of information*, and then followed up with a resume such as the one I will describe immediately below. This would communicate their clarity of intent, thoughtfulness about details and what I call process.

Anyway, in my view, **personal marketing** has *components*:
- **Stuff**: how you present yourself
- **Exposure**: where you present yourself
- **Follow-through**: how you keep track of contacts

Stuff—Social Calling Cards, Photos, Resume, Website

In this day-and-age of computer-generated business cards, it's easy and inexpensive for someone to print a handful of social calling cards that include a photo. (Note: if you *do* include a photo, then I suggest that you use bright-white, glossy card-stock. One of the more challenging aspects of this little project involves getting a nice (clear and uncluttered) photo image. (Technical note: The image will have to be greater than 270dpi to look good; don't bother trying to print off a 72dpi image. You will need a software program to manipulate the image—crop it, lighten or darken it, sharpen it. Ask around: if this is a bit beyond you, ask someone to help.)

Even a simple social calling card without a photo is better than handing out your work/business card. Your professional business card reveals too much about who you are—or who you want others to think you are.

You might wish to develop answers to questions you're likely to be asked:
- Who you are—scene name or real name, but not address. Marital status.
- Means of contact—cell phone? e-mail? Through a Website?
- What you seek—skills, talents, capabilities, duration. Are you looking for a play partner, a third, a weekend event or a 24/7 relationship?
- What you like—your particular kink(s).
- What you seek—the *ideal slave* or *ideal Master* kind of thing.
- Your kink history—are you part of a local group? Do you go to regional conferences?
- Accomplishments—do you speak at BDSM events? Are you recognized for mastery in some BDSM or vanilla arena?

- General overview of your education and work experiences.
- Hobbies/interests?
- Etc.

Next, I suggest that you consider preparing a set of *general* questions that you would ask your potential partner. You can build these from our earlier sections—or simply sit down and start thinking of things you would like to know about this person. Everyone's list would be somewhat different, but here's a start…

- In what areas of life do you consider yourself to be accomplished?
- Have you been particularly successful in your work life? Tell me about that.
- How do you make your money grow?
- Tell me about your relations with your prior spouse(s) and children. Are you close with your family? What about your parents and siblings?
- If time and money were not issues, what new interest areas would you like to explore over the next few years?
- Conceptually, what do you think of playing by SSC (Safe, Sane and Consensual) rules? In your view, what are the strengths and weaknesses of using SSC rules vs. RACK (Risk-Aware Consensual Kink) standards?
- What leisure-time activities do you enjoy?
- What first comes to mind when you see a street person begging for money?
- Tell me something of your spirituality.
- Do you smoke? Drink? Use recreational drugs?
- Do you enjoy meeting new people? How do you do this? If not, why not?
- What volunteer work have you done in the past year or so? Why that group?
- What are your favorite TV shows? Movies? Books?
- How would you describe your spirit of adventure. Examples?
- Ever tried a polyamorous or swinging lifestyle? When were you last tested for STDs and what were the results? What's your position on condom use? (By the way, there are *socially correct* answers to most sex questions—and then there

is the answer that the person has actually worked out for themselves: they may be reluctant to share their real answer.

- Do you have lots of friends? Where do you go to be with them? What kind of activities do you do with them?
- What specific BDSM skills do you have? CBT? Flogging?
- What specific BDSM play do you particularly enjoy or particularly avoid?

These are proxy questions for key issues about kindness, loyalty, personal competence, self-confidence, personal ethics, kink preferences, self-reliance, and so forth. They are only part of your packet of questions. It is up to you to extend this list.

Exposure: Presentation and Follow-Through

Okay, let's presume that you've prepared your bio and thought through questions to ask a prospective respondent or answers to give a prospective inquirer. You've prepared all this *stuff*, now what? Well, you can *advertise*.

- Internet social-networking sites:
    - o FetLife.com, on which you can start your own blog and start to meet those that make comments on your writing
    - o Local club e-groups—although over the past few years most of this has migrated to FetLife
    - o Alt.com—which is really a meat-market for those looking for kinky hookups
    - o collarme.com—for submissives seeking Dom/mes
    - o slave4master.com—for men seeking Masters, mostly gay
- Personals sections of newspapers
- Local munches and meetings

But, advertising may not be enough: you may find it's hard to find a good match. So, while you're waiting, read, go to parties, become known: do volunteer work for your local club. Put yourself out in the world where like-minded folk can find you.

Getting to Know You; Getting to Know All About You

Before you begin a relationship, I **strongly** recommend getting to know the person in a very vanilla way. In the opening stages of your relationship, the D-type should be sharing equal psychological power and authority with the s-type. You're not yet in a negotiated relationship so you're still just two kinky people.

So, take some time with this person in order to figure out how they act and react to unusual situations. Try spending a weekend in a single bed. Make up some reason why it has to be this way, and consider their reactions. Go out slumming for dinner one night, and then have them get seriously dressed up for an upscale dinner another night. See how you guys behave for a weekend at a four-star hotel, then at a one-star hotel. Who is doing the fussing, and what are they fussing about?

I've had any number of instances where my own prejudices rushed to the surface and danced on my head giggling, as I watched someone who certainly didn't *look* the part, exhibit extremely refined manners and behaviors. Similarly, I've had a few experiences where a drop-dead gorgeous and immaculately coiffed *Thing* shattered the magic spell through unrefined speech or action—sending all the magic crashing the ground, flopping and gasping for breath. But, these are **my** hang-ups and not yours. You get to be honest and derive your own self-truths.

Red flags

[Note: Because it's so important—and because it fits so well right here—I'm repeating this section from the first book in this series, *BDSM Mastery: Your comprehensive guide to play, parties, and party protocols.* Frankly, the better you know this material the safer you'll be.]

As I was researching *red flag* behaviors I ran across an exceptional BlogSpot by a woman named Epiphany. She said that Saikiji Kitalpha from *Second Life* was the author and that in the original posting Saikiji had said that anyone could reproduce it but please give her the credit. Saikiji, you did a great job! (What follows is only slightly edited.)

What *red flags* are and why they're important

Red flags are behavioral warning signs that something is not quite right. These behaviors are not specific to any gender, sexual orientation, or relationship structure. While these warning flags apply equally to straight folk and kinky folk, you probably have a statistically greater chance of finding some disturbed folk in our BDSM world, simply because of what it is that we do to amuse ourselves. Predators can hide more easily, here.

Now, someone with one, two, or five of these behaviors may raise your eyebrow, but when you find groups of repeating, negative behaviors, you'll want to be on alert. The more of these behaviors someone exhibits, the stronger the chance that something is psychologically wrong with them. Since *something wrong with them* can mean a lot of trouble for you, this is an important section of this book.

My strong message to you is this: Take your time in establishing new relationships, for it may take time for these behaviors or patterns to emerge. When you see these behaviors, I'd suggest that you slow down or even stop the relationship in order to assess your situation. Generally, the more of these behaviors you observe in a person (and the more often you see them and the quicker they emerge in a new relationship), the more you are at risk for being emotionally and/or physically harmed by this person.

Categorized list of potentially alarming behaviors

Before you start reading these lists, please recognize that while you may find some of these behaviors in most people, you won't find clusters of them in people who are psychologically and emotionally safe and stable. If you find yourself thinking that these behaviors really describe a friend of yours (even a spouse), you may wish to ask yourself whether this friend (or spouse) is really good for you.

A caution: not all of us are born with neuro-typical brain wiring. A substantial (and apparently growing) number of us (myself included) fall somewhere on the Autism spectrum and exhibit certain unusual social behaviors. You might wish to familiarize yourself with Autism Spectrum Disorder traits, as many of us exhibit social oddness that can be off-putting at best and alarming at worst. But that's different than being dangerous for you, and that's what this section is about.

Tries to isolate you:
- Tries to limit your access to others in your life—friends, family, and BDSM community.
- Forbids contact with others or undermines relationships or activities.
- Is negative and unsupportive of your other (established) relationships.
- Monitors your communications (e-mails, phone calls, chats).
- May want you to quit your job or give up your car or telephone or control your finances.
- Monitors your activities; demands to know where you've been and who you've been with—often in an accusatory manner.
- Habitually calls and/or visits unexpectedly.
- Refuses to allow you a safe-call.
- Becomes angry if you question them or show signs of independence or strength.

Is deceptive:
- Is reluctant to give you personal and factual information about themselves.
- Refuses to give their marital status when asked before a first meeting.
- Gives inconsistent or conflicting information or details about themselves or past events.
- Has very limited times/placeSMethods where you are able to contact them and gets angry if you try to make contact outside of those conditions.
- Does not give you their home or work phone numbers at the appropriate time.
- Has multiple online identities for interacting within the same communities.

- Cheats on you.
- Gives the impression of being very successful without any evidence of real success.
- Disappears from communication for days or weeks at a time without explanation.
- Is evasive about their activities, especially unexplained absences.
- Only interacts with you in a kinky or sexual manner—as if role-playing.
- Will not have normal everyday vanilla conversations.

Behaves oddly:
- Your friends warn you against the person.
- Is critical of the public BDSM community and will not participate in BDSM clubSMunches/parties.
- Is critical of many respected members of the BDSM community and has interpersonal conflicts with other BDSM-ers.
- Has no apparent BDSM references or friends you can talk to, and becomes angry, changes the topic, answers questions with questions, or ends the conversation when you ask personal questions or ask for references.
- May give you names of friends, but you can't verify that they even exist: you suspect that he made up the names.
- Has bad or no relationship with their biological family.

Seems insecure:
- Often exaggerates.
- Deflects blame to others for things going wrong and resorts to extreme measures to prove that they, themselves, are not at fault.
- Does not take personal responsibility when things go badly; will not acknowledge their own mistakes.
- Their apologies feel insincere, phony, or are insulting.
- Puts you down in front of others.
- Is constantly comparing themselves to others.
- Brags excessively about their experience, scene credentials, mastery, or training.

- Engages in scene name-dropping.
- Avoids discussing what your possible future relationship could be like. Tries to keep you in the dark about what might happen next in the relationship.
- Seems not to reveal their emotional side; hides their vulnerabilities or behaves in an emotionless manner.
- Hides behind their D/s authority; demands that their authority not be questioned.

Is disrespectful:
- Does not respect your feelings, rights, or opinions.
- Is rude to public servers such as waitresses, cashiers, and janitors.
- Displays little concern or awareness of the feelings or needs of others.
- Never/seldom says *thank you, excuse me* or *I am sorry* to anyone.
- Exhibits obvious and excessive displays of impatience.
- Believe that they deserve some particular reward or benefit even at the expense of others.

Is manipulative:
- Tries to make you feel guilty for not being *good enough*.
- Says that you are not a *true* sub/slave/Dom (or Domme).
- Belittles your ideas.
- Blames you for their own hurt feelings and anger outbursts.
- Blames you for all relationship problems.
- Yells or threatens to withdraw their love/leave you if you do not do as they wish.

Is inconsistent:
- Does not keep their word; breaks promises.
- Makes plans with you, then makes excuses for changing those plans.
- Treats you lovingly and respectfully one day and then harshly and accusingly the next.
- Goes through extreme highs (behaving with great kindness) and pronounced lows (behaving with cruelty), almost as though they are two distinctly different people.

Is domineering:
- Pressures you into doing things you do not want to do.
- Does not respect your limits, negotiations, or contracts.
- Pushes you too quickly into a D/s or M/s or poly relationship.
- Pushes you into a sexual relationship too fast.
- Overly demanding of your time; must be the center of your attention.
- Insists safewords/safe-calls are not necessary.

Is intemperate:
- Conspicuous consumption: spends money largely and inappropriately on luxury items.
- Abuses alcohol or other drugs.
- Gambles excessively.
- Constantly asks for money or material goods from you or others.
- Falls in love with you way too fast; swears undying love before even meeting you.
- Begins saying things like, *I can't live without you,* or *Do what you want with me,* or *I don't have any limits.*
- Deliberately says or does things that result in getting themselves hurt.

Is temperamental:
- Loses control of their emotions in arguments. Raises their voice, yells, calls you names, blames you for things they did.
- Uses force or violence to solve problems.
- Punches walls or throws things when upset.
- Turns on their peers, going quickly from *best friend* to *arch enemy*, often for trivial or imagined reasons.
- Speaks badly of others, particularly of people with whom they once were good friends.
- Displays a disproportionately negative reaction to being told *no*.
- Holds excessive grudges against others and goes to great lengths to get revenge on people.
- Threatens suicide or other forms of self-harm.
- Hypersensitive and easily upset by annoyances that are part of daily life.

Has certain established behaviors:
- They, themselves, were victims of abuse. (Their abuse may be a learned behavior.)
- May exhibit cruel behavior towards animals.
- Might admit to hitting a partner in the past, but claims the partner made them do it.

Quite a list. And it brings us neatly to the next section.

Don't get involved with someone who wants to break you

Occasionally, someone asks me how to psychologically break down a submissive in order to build the person back up in ways they wish. Every so often—particularly on the less-sophisticated Internet hookup sites—you'll find ads for people seeking to be *broken*. I strongly suspect that most of these people are living in the Internet world of fantasy-BDSM, but who knows? Perhaps they've just seen movies (such as The Pet) and/or read fiction about using physical force and terror to strip a person's ego-defenses in order to retrain them to behave and react exactly as the trainer wishes them to.

Couple of things. First, psychological brainwashing is, by definition, non-consensual. Second, even if they were a licensed and credentialed psychologist or psychiatrist, it is unethical to *break* someone like that. Those professions are for healing, not molding someone to their own will.

Please be clear: breaking—the way I'm using it—is different than *behavior modification*. As few people know much about psychology, many new Tops and bottoms ask these kinds of *breaking* questions because it's part of the stereotype that BDSM is about breaking someone's spirit/will, presumably based on the other stereotype that BDSM is about pain/punishment.

Someone who is considering engaging in an unsafe non-consensual activity with another person either:
- Realizes the risks and is willing to proceed anyway (suggesting sadistic behavior that may turn out to include criminal intent), or

- Does not understand or appreciate what they are contemplating, and thus has an altered sense of reality— which is a classic definition of insanity.

Now, another caution: Having an *altered sense of reality* may be very hard to ascertain initially, particularly if someone is well-versed in the jargon of our culture. As a person may not come right out and tell you their purposes, you can refer to the previous lists of potentially alarming behaviors as indications that you're with a truly dangerous person.

Starting a New Relationship— a Period of Being Crazy

For many people, the first several months of a new relationship are characterized by a wild emotional high. The new partner is heaven-sent. The new partner is the most amazing surprise you've ever had. The new partner does everything perfectly. The new partner is so smart, so talented, so wise. The new partner, the new partner, the new partner. Jay Wiseman tells me that in polyamorous circles, this is known NRE—New Relationship Energy: he calls it *the three month crazies.*

That's why most Seniors that you ask will advise you to **slow down**. Take it easy. Don't rush. Get to know the person as a person. That's why training contracts are often 3-4 months long. You have to see how the new partner looks and behaves in **six** months.

Cautionary Indications About D- or s- Types

There are some early warning signs of trouble both for D-types and for s-types in our community. In the most general way, established BDSMers become concerned when someone really new to the scene commits to someone who is also new to the scene. Blind-leading-the-blind and all that. Newcomers of all persuasions are encouraged to spend your first year or so learning about BDSM before adding in the complexity that goes with a relationship.

When it comes to questionable D-type behavior, one imagines the person pushing limits, not listening to the s-type's needs, or sexually using the new s-type who is emotionally off-balance because of the tremendously new and unusual experiences afforded by this lifestyle. However, when it comes to questionable s-type behavior one thinks of drama queens, financial predators, and emotionally broken people.

Here are some other areas to consider when evaluating a prospective partner:

- **Hasn't done their homework:** Your new partner has accepted this relationship with you, but has NOT checked YOUR reputation within your local BDSM community. If your potential partner hasn't checked *you* out, they may be unusually naïve or so new to the community that they don't know *how* to check you out. Or, they may be a little arrogant and feel that they can discern all your strengths and weaknesses on their own. This is not likely to be true, is it?
- **Has *issues* that are not easy to evaluate:** Your new partner may be addicted to drugs, alcohol, sex, pain, food, etc. While active additions are be pretty self-evident, addictive behavior patterns can be hidden and/or misinterpreted by those not trained to recognize them. But, people with active or prior addictions have certain common characteristics that can include stunted emotional development—so, you may wish to do some research into *addictive behavior* before getting too heavily involved with our community. Anyway, it's a good piece of general knowledge to have.
- **Secretive:** Your new partner won't account for a block of time that has disappeared. He/she keeps ducking and weaving when asked the simple question: "Where were you?" (Warning: she/he may have been out finding you a surprise birthday present—so, be careful about forcing an answer.)
- **Hidden behavior:** The s-type keeps an online journal (blog) that you either don't know about or don't monitor on the grounds that it is trivial. (I know of a case where a Dom chose not to monitor his submissive's blog. As it happened, she was a disturbed person and was broadcasting extremely private and negative half-truths about him. These unchallenged

fabrications went around the submissives' network like wildfire and caused him to be declared *persona non grata* in a number of local clubs.)

- **Drama-prone:** Your new slave has frequent personal crises beyond the normal or average that could be expected in any life. This could indicate that this person may—through their personal choices—bring these problems upon themselves. I doubt that you will enjoy being along for that ride.

- **Moody:** Your new partner seems to have dramatic mood swings: nice and pleasant most of the time, then aggressive and abusive without warning. Same comment as above: this is not normal and you will probably not enjoy being along for that ride.

- **Passive/aggressive behavior:** He/she keeps saying "yes," yet your requests are ignored or poorly completed. Outward behaviors such as these have deep roots. It's not likely you will be able to do something with a fully-grown adult who exhibits them.

- **Warnings from others:** People seem to be trying to tell you something about your slave candidate, but you can't quite understand what they're getting at. You sense that you're being offered a warning, but you bristle, and the other person retreats. All I can say to this is: suppress your knee-jerk defense of the slave candidate and listen.

- **Refusal to negotiate:** Your slave-to-be doesn't want to have a formal negotiation and contract with you on the grounds that this is a Master/slave relationship, and as Master, you surely know how to treat him/her, and you only need to know that he/she wants to serve you. Ummmm, errrrr this is, perhaps, an Internet person? Knowing, understanding, and communicating your limits and needs will help prevent abuses of trust.

So, let's say that NO *red flags* have surfaced—or at least not enough to slow you down very much. The two of you are ready to start negotiating the terms and conditions of your relationship. For many of you, that means a **contract.**

Chapter 3—Finding a Partner

Or does it?

And, what does a contract cover, anyway?

Well, that's were we're going in the next Chapter.

Chapter 4
Roles Within Relationships

As I say repeatedly, this is the world where you can explore magic; this is a world where there is more going on than meets the eye. This is a world that takes some time to learn and even longer to understand. This is a world where you have to master a knowledge base in addition to physical and social skills before you can grow to understand why so many people are drawn to it. To repeat Tristan Taormino's comment from her book *The Ultimate Guide to Kink: BDSM, Role Play and the Erotic Edge*: "This is the world of sex geeks: we actually go to classes and read books on this stuff. Proof: you're reading this book."

Why speak about roles?

Words explain concepts. To the extent that you misunderstand a word (or the way someone is using it), you risk misunderstanding the concept that word represents. Since people use concepts to interpret the world around them, I am going to spend some time in this chapter carefully explaining the words that make up the concepts that in turn constitute one's understanding the various *roles* you can play within your relationships. I'm spending time on this topic because many newcomers get lost when it comes to knowing who they are (or who they may wish to become) in this world of alternative sexuality.

In the BDSM culture, some words may be used somewhat differently (and with more precision) than you may be used to. More than that, some of these words, terms, and concepts have slightly different meanings in different parts of this country and are often interpreted slightly differently among the various BDSM sub-subcultures, themselves.

While there aren't *absolute* definitions for these terms, there is some general agreement about what these terms mean: you'll need to know these words in order to be able to converse intelligently with other BDSMers.

Because these words are so important, I encourage you to read this chapter very carefully.

As a starting point, certain words are used to describe how people *present* themselves to others, while other words describe how people *relate* to one another. Certain words are used to describe *motivations* underlying activities, while other words describe the *activities* themselves. Some will refer to themselves as a Dominant, a Master, or an Owner. Some will refer to themselves as a slave, a submissive, a toy, or a pet. Some will represent themselves as a boy, a boi, a girl, a gurl, or a babygirl—all subtly different. But beware: these terms represent only a starting point to discuss a topic and not some standard against which you judge other people.

Translation: the way someone self-describes is rather like telling someone which State you live in. You'll understand that someone from Southern California probably has a little different world-view than someone from Northern Michigan, but the subtleties may take some time to work out. Even if they say they're from Southern California and you've been there, you still don't know whether they grew up out in the Mojave Dessert or in downtown LA. Just because someone self-describes as a babygirl does not mean that you know what that means to them in the context of their relationship.

As you learn more about BDSM and get to know people better, you will learn not to be too surprised to discover unusual personality and role complexities. You'll learn not to react visibly when you first realize that the Master you see with a slave actually has a Master of his or her own. You'll come to understand how the person you know as the strongly dominant partner can also be the masochistic bottom in the relationship. And I'm not even going near the topic of genetic females who wish to be addressed as *Sir*.

Role identification can get confusing quickly.

Oh, before you tackle the rest of this chapter, let me mention that the discussion of how these words/terms work comes later. I realize that I've been hinting about many of these terms repeatedly up to this point. Here, though, I'm going into more detail and will often compare and contrast one term or set of terms with others, so please bear with me. As I keep saying, this is a complex world and the meanings of most of the commonly used words carry subtlety and connotation that can make a great deal of difference when it comes to structuring your personal relationship. This is a fluid world and the details of relationships result from the blending of individual personalities. In the end, there is no one true way. There is no such thing and never will be.

About being a Dom or sub

Being dominant isn't about being domineering or being aggressive, it's about taking and maintaining control. How you do that depends upon your personality and the personality of those with whom you're interacting. Even during a play scene, the key concepts are *focus*, *intent* and *skill*, not aggression.

Being submissive isn't about being passive or shy, it's about surrendering physical and psychological control to another. Being submissive is about giving yourself to another and allowing them to do as they wish—within the negotiated bounds of that play or relationship. At no time is *being a submissive* about being a doormat.

Notes about trying to define personal roles. Although the following definitions (descriptions) sound fairly neat and clean, it's not that way in real life. Some s-types identify as *submissive* even though they have surrendered authority over themselves to their Dom/me. While they refer to themselves as *submissives*, their relationship structure appears to others to be closer to *slave* than to *sub*. Similarly, the Dom/mes in control of such s-types do not consistently refer to themselves as *Master*. This rich complexity of relationship structures and roles—this land of flexibility and possibility—makes the BDSM world hard to understand yet lots of fun to live in.

Here is a graduate-school level synopsis of this discussion (at least my version of it): the words *dominant* and *submissive* describe aspects of one's personality; *slave* or *property* describes roles one can assume whether one has a dominant or submissive personality. The *slave* or *property* roles have to do with *slaveheart* or service—and your choice about how you wish to behave around a particular person/partner. This gets confusing, because *to have a submissive personality* gets mixed up with the role of *being the subordinate partner*. There are certainly cases where a self-identified dominant has chosen to be the subordinate partner in a relationship. *That does not make them a submissive person.* In the terminology of Chris M. Lyon this makes them the *supportive* (as opposed to *submissive*) partner. (Chris M. Lyon is the author of the fabulously insightful book: *Leading and Supportive Love: the Truth About Dominant and Submissive Relationships.*)

In my world, the *behaviors* and *actions* of a person filling the *submissive* role in a D/s structure can be almost indistinguishable from a person filling the *slave* role in an M/s structure. The key issues:
- First, while the submissive has the authority to negotiate areas where they retain personal authority and control, the slave will not;
- Second, D/s structures tend to have far fewer and less formal protocols than M/s structures;
- Third, unlike D/s structures, M/s structures tend to start out with contracts between the two parties.
- Fourth, and with some trepidation, I'll add a key issue that exists more in the Leather world than in the BDSM world:

a *Master* must be a good leader but may or may not have a very dominant personality while a *dominant* in a D/s relationship is clearly a person with a dominant personality—and may or may not be a good leader (they may be more of a bully than a true leader—leading by fear rather than by inspiration).

Dominance as a concept

What is dominance? According to Webster Online, personal dominance relates to one's relative position in a social hierarchy and describes the exercise of power or influence over others. Thus, one "submissive" directing another "submissive" would be acting as a dominant. In the most general sense, dominance appears on two ways. First, it can be expressed as role-play (one partner is consensually empowered to *dominate* and the other partner empowered to submit) for the limited purpose of sado-masochistic or sexual games. Second, it can reflect deep-seated personality traits that influence most aspects of person's life.

What is it to *be* a Dominant? One expresses dominance through one's ability to project authority. Thus, the dominant Army Lieutenant, can easily project authority over those of lesser rank, yet express subordinance (as opposed to submissiveness) to those of greater rank. In our BDSM culture, a person serving as the decision-maker in a scene or relationship is referred to in the shortened form of "Dom" (male) or "Domme" (female). (By the way, these words are pronounced the same way. Domme is *not* pronounced *dom-ay*: it's not French.) In the case of D/s or M/s structures, the Dom/me expresses their dominance through appropriate leadership.

Within our culture, dominance is usually viewed as a skill that evolves and develops with practice and application. (By the way, this motivation is the defining difference between *dominance* and *domineering*.) Typically, the Dom/me in a long-term relationship strives to support their submissive's personal goals in exchange for service. If successful, the Dom/me is rewarded by the submissive's choice to stay with them in service and devotion.

Being Dom/me versus being domineering. Dominance through appropriate leadership is vastly different than dominance through force or threat of force, bullying or nagging (coercion). A Dom/me *accepts* service, a bully/bitch *expects* service. Someone who is *domineering* seeks to keep their partner in a "one-down" position and under their close control. Often, this form of oppressive control stems from a personal fear of being rejected or upstaged. It is negative motivation leading to even more negative outcomes.

How is a Dom/me different than a Top? A *Top* is simply the person doing the action in an SM scene. The word carries no D/s significance. A Dom/me *controls* the SM scene or relationship, exercising authority over their partner(s). Depending upon the Top's personality and the overall intent of the SM scene, he/she may use a pre-scene ritual during which the Top takes the submissive's "power" of personal control to use as they (the Dom/me) sees fit. Such power exchange rituals usually augment a scene's intensity.

How is a D/s Dominant different than an M/s *Leader*? (This is a semantics discussion that may not make much sense until you've had a bit more experience.) BDSM relationships tend to produce Dominant/submissive pairings that focus on *activities* (such as SM play and sex). At the risk of igniting a firestorm of controversy, it is my considered opinion that most D/s structures have the Dom/me involved with micromanaging the submissive person and focused on controlling that person. It is my further opinion that a Master in an M/s relationship is focused on long-range leadership, guidance, and expressing personal authority. D/s is what you do; M/s is who you are. In terms of the two (or more) people involved, D/s is inward looking; M/s is outward looking. D/s is about what the submissive can do for the Dom/me; M/s is about who the two of you are in the larger world. One is not better than the other, these are simply different paths. In choosing a relationship partner, I urge you to understand this distinction and make sure that the person with whom you're partnering shares your vision and is a correct match for your choice.

How does one learn to be a Dom/me? Here is a story of unknown origins that helps to answer this question: A man once asked Mozart how to write a symphony. Mozart told him to study at the conservatory for six or eight years, then apprentice with a composer for four or five more years, then begin writing a few sonatas, pieces for string quartets, piano concertos, etc. and in another four or five years he would be ready to try a full symphony. The man said, "But Mozart, didn't your write a symphony at age eight?" Mozart replied, "Yes, but I didn't have to ask how."

The words "dominance" and "submission" occupy opposite ends of a sliding personality scale that

How is a Domme different from a Pro-Domme or Dominatrix?
The word "Domme" has evolved to mean a female dominant who participates in BDSM activities as a lifestyle choice. Should they make a business out of BDSM (possibly combined with sex) and get paid for Topping people (usually men), they are then referred to as professional Dommes, or Pro-Dommes. For most people, the words Pro-Domme and Dominatrix are interchangeable. Some Pro-Dommes are also "lifestyle Dommes." It is not unusual to discover that a Pro-Domme is not a dominant in other aspects of their life: it's a business and they deliver what their clients want when it's wanted.

Dominant roles in a relationship.

Some people use dominance and submission in their relationship structure as a way of expressing the power-imbalance: the submissive follows the dominant's leadership. (Note: there is no correlation between being a dominant person and being a sadist or masochist— these are totally different topics.)

In the broadest sense, a D-type is a **leader** and an s-type is a **follower**. The leader says, "Do X" and the follower says: "Yes, Sir." Relationships get into trouble when something comes up that the D-type interprets as a threat to their leadership. Behavior that challenges the D-type's leadership or authority are potentially threatening and destabilizing to the relationship. These "relationship hick-ups" are the source of friction and upset and send the signal that in some way, the s-type's needs are not being met.

In the "not-vanilla" world of alternative relationships, there are four very broad groupings of people who lead relationships. As you might expect, there are fundamental differences between these four types of leaders: their purposes are different. As personal genders have no bearing on the roles, please feel free to substitute genders to fit your own world:

- a **Dom** may be paired with a submissive in a D/s relationship structure;
- a **Daddy** may have a little girl
- a **Master** may have a slave
- an **Owner** may have property

Dominant: The Dom/me in a D/s relationship has strong *influence* over their s-type. The D-type may actually have authority over certain aspects of the s-type's world, but that *authority* is not absolute (as it is in M/s structures). Commonly, there are limits placed on the D-type's authority over the s-type's work, spiritual beliefs, education, and relationships with biological family. One often hears the words "control" and "punishment" used in D/s relationships. In most D/s relationships, the D-type makes decisions about everything from what their submissive will wear and eat to how they use their free time. The amount of control that the submissive cedes to the dominant varies a great deal and defines the relationship.

The Dom/mes are usually seeking service and sexual access from the submissive, they are seldom seeking to change their s-type very much. D/s relationships are essentially vanilla "boyfriend/girlfriend" structures that include SM sex plus a much more clearly defined leader/follower structure. Frequently, Dom/mes concentrate on helping the s-type to expand the sub's existing strengths under their guidance and vision. In this light, Dom/mes may focus on coaxing the s-type to find their own Path in the world; Dom/mes do not usually have the degree of authority required to *require* the s-type to change Paths.

Daddy or Mommy: A dominant person—usually but not necessarily kinky—who likes being a parent figure. A *Daddy* differs from a *Master* in that they offer a more nurturing and supportive model. A Daddy knows the value of discipline, though at times his soft heart gets the best of him. *Mommy* roles are parallel.

Master: This word means so many things to so many people that I'm at something of a loss how to explain it without upsetting some segment of the BDSM world. It seems people sort through the various uses of the word and choose the definition that works best for them. In perhaps the broadest sense, people seem to use the word *Master* in one of three ways:

- As an earned rank, *Master* recognizes the contributions of those who are senior in the community. In that sense, males or females use *Master* much as a rank of *Major* would apply to either gender. You may find that other senior members of the community refer to them using the *Master* honorific before their name (Master Bill).
- As a relationship role indicator, the word signifies that a man or woman is the *Master* of someone else, often pursuant to a negotiated contract. You may find that only people who serve this person refer to him/her as *Master*. Others may refer to him as *Sir* or her as *Ma'am*.
- As a recognition of mastery over a particular skill, as in *whip master*.

Overall, exerting mastery over another is viewed as an extremely serious and sobering responsibility. At least in theory, one is not supposed to try to *Master* another until they have mastered themselves and have learned to act consistently with purpose, authority, wisdom, and compassion. In some communities, one is not publically recognized as a Master (as in, who is to judge?) until a senior Master so recognizes you in a public *capping ceremony*. In other communities, though, you buy yourself a Master's Cover and see whether anyone challenges you for having done so.

Unlike Dominant/submissive structures that focus on *activities* (such as SM play), M/s is much more about Superior/subordinate structures that focus on who each of you are in terms of the relationship. While not the subject of this book, a Master's responsibility to a slave involves such things as:

- Maintaining and protecting the trust given to him/her by the slave's submission.
- Being clear about the terms and conditions of the slave's

service, including restrictions on the slave's activities and Master's rights to use the slave.

- Ensuring the slave's physical, social, emotional, spiritual and financial wellbeing.
- Providing whatever training, direction and guidance is necessary to develop the slave to his/her true potential.
- Establishing and maintaining effective lines of communication with the slave.
- Exercising care and sound judgment in the relationship, as the slave's condition and conduct reflects upon the Master and his/her House.

Owner: The term *Owner* is starting to be used to describe a permanent M/s relationship based on a profound exchange of profound vows. There seems to be a growing trend to pair the title *Owner* with the word *property* rather than *slave*. The Owner pledges to take care of his/her property and keep it in good running order and the person agreeing to become property pledges to obey and to serve his/her Owner. Period. Permanently. No written contract.

There is an interesting subtlety that arises concerning the Owner's versus the Master's degree of authority over the *property* or the *slave*. While a Master has absolute and virtually total authority over a slave and is well within his/her power to require the slave to change fundamental aspects of its life or behavior or likes/dislikes, it's not quite so clear that someone serving as *property* has actually agreed to permit themselves to be radically changed. As I said in the prior paragraph, an Owner pledges to take care of their property: by implication, the property is seeking an Owner to serve in exchange for being maintained. That is a fairly passive state and it differs from a slave state. In most M/s relationships, slave is expected to "write a blank check" to their Master and "say 'yes' before the question is asked" concerning any of Master's wishes.

Trainer: A dominant who is primarily concerned about *teaching systems* that improve and refine a slave's skill set—such as puppy skills or pony skills. You may hear *Trainer* used as a title, as in *Trainer Carolyn*.

submission as a concept

What is submission? According to Webster Online, *submission* describes the state of being obedient; the act of accepting the authority or control of someone else. According to Dictionary.com, *submission* means:

- to yield oneself to the power or authority of another: to submit to a conqueror.
- to allow oneself to be subjected to some kind of treatment: to submit to chemotherapy.
- to defer to another's judgment, opinion, decision, etc.: I submit to your superior judgment.

What is it to *be* a submissive? Ah, well, that depends upon who you are as an adult and the "chemistry" between you and your Dom/me as much as it depends upon your personal ideas about how a submissive person should act.

Perhaps it's easier for me to tell you what it is not. It is *not* an abdication of personal responsibility or a total deferral to the Dom/me. A person who checks their brain at the door is not likely to be accepted into a long-term D/s unless the Dom/me is looking for someone so weak-willed that they will put up with abuse. A sub that over-relies on the well-intentioned Dom/me's leadership and initiative will end up with a burned-out Dom/me. The "witless sub" model requires far more work from the Dom/me than most will tolerate: most Dom/mes consider "do-me" or "high-maintenance" subs to be manipulating the relationship from the bottom and won't put up with it. (A "do-me" person wants to be the center of attention and willingly gives their body to be pleasured: they are much less willing to *do* the pleasuring (or *do* the housework) without *being* themselves pleasured. In a general sense, they maintain a "what's in it for me" attitude. *High-maintenance* is divided into two dimensions: physical and emotional. The former requires lots of expensive items to make their life work the way they wish; the latter requires nearly constant personal affirmation and encouragement to overcome deep-seeded insecurities and poor self-esteem.)

How is the word "subordinate" different from "submissive?" Here is how the *Oxford English Dictionary* defines *subordinate*: (n) "Of a person or body of persons belonging to an inferior rank, grade, class, or order and hence dependent upon the authority or power of another."

The subordinate person is in the *following* position; this is the person taking orders. However, the fact that they are following orders does not make them a submissive person: A macho prisoner who terrorizes and dominates other inmates is still subordinate to the lowest-ranked prison guard. Whether one is in the superior or subordinate position depends upon specific situations and is not related to whether one has a dominant or submissive personality.

I'll tell you up-front: this is a concept that applies to M/s, rather than in D/s relationships. I'm bringing it up in this book so you will begin to realize some of the fundamental differences between how D/s and M/s relationships work. Once you understand that slaves are *subordinates* rather than *submissives* you'll then begin to understand why many slaves seem to have much more latitude than submissives when it comes to expressing elements of their own dominance while taking responsibility for their supportive role in the relationship.

If you would like to read more about M/s structures, I refer you to our parallel series of books on *Master/slave Mastery*.

submissive roles in a relationship

In a relationship, the "sub" is the person who chooses at certain times and with certain conditions to submit to the will of their partner. The conditions typically including terms of service, length of service, areas of the submissives' life the Dominant does *not* get to control, the hard and soft limits when they play or just interact, and the safewords they will use when scening. Although it is counterintuitive, the submissive has some degree of control over an SM play scene through safewords—at least until they enter subspace.

In a general way, submissives are wholly formed people who maintain personal authority over (and responsibility for) themselves. Submissives in a relationship retain enough personal authority to say "no" to their Dom/me. (That is generally not the case for slaves: slaves are usually considered to be their Master's property.) In the BDSM world, *submission* is not taken from an unwilling person, but is given as part of a negotiated exchange of power between those involved.

Being a submissive: The behavior of *submission* appears superficially to be the opposite of *domination,* and (also superficially) it appears to be *passive*—simply taking orders or direction from a Dominant and completing tasks to their liking. This misperception sucks all kinds of people into our lifestyle: from D-types who want free maid and sex service from someone who won't talk back, to s-types with low self-esteem who will do about anything simply to have someone who seems to care about them.

In the D/s world, some submissives stand out in their service. They are prized by Dominants and admired by other submissives. Their difference is evident to those who have been around even for a relatively short time. Their difference is not in physical looks, clothing, age, or body type; their difference is in their *character.* And, *character* is a combination of *bearing* (itself a blend of moral/ethical strength plus intelligently applied common sense) combined with *devotion* and *submission.*

The exceptional sub does not merely comply with orders, but has learned how to anticipate and meet their Dom/me's wants and needs. This learning can be formal (focused education or professional development) or informal (paying attention to how you dress, your health, your physical fitness, or by mastering the arts of submission and service—what I call "courtesan services").

How is a little different than a babygirl? Within the context of a BDSM relationship, a *little* is someone (usually but not necessarily an s-type) that enjoys spending time being a younger age. Commonly, *littles* enjoy age play and childish behaviors that help them to enjoy the opportunity to explore their younger selves. I've met "littles" who were kindergarten age, school age, and just entering puberty. I've met people of both genders whom I've normally considered to be Dom/mes that were sitting on the floor with crayons and coloring books. In a general sense, people go into "little-headspace" to step out of their roles within their D/s structure—it's playtime.

A *babygirl* doesn't have to be of a "baby" age. A Daddy Dom might refer to his submissive as his babygirl, even though she doesn't exhibit "little" behavior. Both the *littles* and *babygirl* roles are intended to be part of a more nurturing and supportive relationship dynamic than you'd usually find with submissive or slave roles in D/s or M/s structures. I know of a number of M/s and D/s couples in which the s-type has a way of signaling their need to drop in to "little-headspace;" the D-type knows to change their own interaction styles to match their partner's needs during those times.

From my limited sampling of littles and babygirls, I have the impression that they don't have sex while in that headspace unless they are also involved in role-playing *incest play*. In that case, the relationship is most often referred to as "Daddy/daughter" rather than "Daddy/girl."

What is a slave? A slave is a person of either gender who falls somewhere on the dominance-submission scale who has transferred authority over him/herself to another. In a general sense, the distinction between a *submissive* and *slave* focuses on whether the person retains any personal authority and/or retains any meaningful decision-making capabilities or surrenders such authority to someone else. Also, play rules are usually different for slaves, as they lack the personal authority to tell their Master to stop a scene. While all slaves are subordinate to their Masters, there is no requirement for the slave to be particularly submissive. In the Master/slave culture, the core values are *service* and *obedience*, not submission.

The "slave" role is unique within the overall BDSM culture: once the person has accepted its status as *slave*, it no longer has personal authority other than to leave the relationship. In practical matters, this means that if Master determines that it is in the best interest of the slave to quit its job or obtain more/different education, or change fundamental aspects of the way slave speaks or interacts with others, the slave is obliged to comply. To use SlaveMaster's phrase from the Butchmann's Experience: Master is responsible for slave's "can'ts," slave is responsible for slave's "won'ts." At issue: if a slave is capable of carrying out an order and willfully declines to do so, slave has essentially withdrawn from the relationship, for slave has now broken the basis of the relationship—to serve and to obey.

What is it to be considered property? A person who has entered into an Owner/property relationship structure in the subordinate role. Some people consider a person serving as *property* to be slightly different from a person serving as *slave*. In the most general sense, Owner/property structures seem to have fewer formal protocols, whereas *slave* in a Master/slave environment is likely to have a great number of speech, dress, and behavior protocols.

As PhoenixRed has mentioned, both words are emotionally charged in the U.S. Some people dislike using the word *slave* because it carries such a cultural shame from the Civil War era, yet some people dislike using the word *property* because it suggests dehumanizing and objectifying someone. (Historically, *property* tends to be associated with the non-consensual form of slavery that implies no rights or limits—such as Roman slavery or Negros in the South.)

Littles, submissives, slaves, and property are all distinct roles descriptors, but actual people differ in countless ways. Each relationship is different and one's conduct changes when we change to a new relationship with someone. Whether one considers oneself to be a *submissive*, a *little*, a *slave*, or *property* is partly a matter of personal choice and partly a matter of loosely observed definitions.

About switches

The word "switch" is used in two quite different ways: a physical switch and a psychological switch.

Physical switches–versatile: Physical switches, called "versatile" within the gay Leather community, are people who sometimes play as Tops and sometimes play as bottoms. There is no particular negative association with being a physical switch (as there is with being a psychological switch).

Psychological switchs: A psychological switch (such as myself) will lead a relationship as the dominant partner or serve in a relationship as the subordinate partner depending upon the psychological chemistry between the people involved. Few men will admit to being a psychological switch, as they encounter quite a bit of negative bias within the community. Generally, switches are discounted by Doms as being too weak-willed (indecisive) to make up their minds.

This discussion about bias against switches brings up an even more controversial topic: sex-role bias within our community. For a variety of interesting historical reasons, Western civilization contains a built-in bias that views men as dominant and women as submissive—more than simply subordinate. As followers, s-type people are sometimes judged by Dominants (usually Dominants of the male persuasion) as being of less value/worth as people than D-types. This bias is sometimes seen in the workplace where men are paid more than women holding the same job with the same seniority; this bias sometimes plays out both in work and social settings when a woman's suggestion on some topic is discounted or ignored until expressed (a bit later) by a man.

In fact, this last example can creep into relationships in nearly the same form. Women frequently comment about how frustrating it can be when their partner discounts or ignores their advice/suggestion but then comes up with the same idea some time later—as if it was their own idea.

Now—the general message is this: if you're the D-type and you're leading an s-type and you are hearing them say things like: "Yes, I told you that two days ago; you never pay attention to what I say," your relationship will improve if you start paying attention to what they're saying. But there is a more specific message that relates to our BDSM world: if you're setting up a play scene and your partner makes a comment or observation concerning set-up or equipment safety, you'd best pay *very close attention*. This is not a setting where you're going to want to hear her later say: "Yes, I told you twice that the third anchoring cable seemed loose."

In our kinky world, some Dominants discount the opinions, views, and actions of submissive **men** even more than they do for submissive women. It can be hard to get much traction in this community if you are known to be a male s-type in the same way that many FemDommes find it hard to interact smoothly with Doms who are unused to considering women to be their intellectual equals. In this latter case, conversations tend to stall when the Dom appears to discount or speak down to the Domme. Women, being used to this behavior, usually simply switches to their, "Oh, I'm speaking with an asshole" communications style.

Sexual relationship roles

Sex: Vanilla vs. BDSM.
Vanilla is the term BDSMers use for those who do not practice BDSM sex. It's not a pejorative term, simply a descriptor. While vanilla sex can be lots of fun and involve a playful spanking or two (or a few hard swats during sex, or one partner tying the other partner up with silk scarves and neckties to spice up their sex life), the emphasis is exactly as one sees in the vast majority of porn movies: oral sex, fingering, and intercourse. In vanilla sex, additional acts such as spanking, caning, or bondage are not *purposefully* used to heighten the receiver's erotic/emotional state. There is wider, deeper, and richer knowledge about ways to sexually stimulate a partner in BDSM sex than in vanilla sex.

In BDSM, arousal techniques may involve: some mix of:
- Tools/toys (vibrators, floggers, canes, dildos, electrical stimulation, fire play, etc)
- SM techniques (where you use the equipment, how you use the equipment, the sequencing of which equipment you use, etc)
- Roles (Teacher/student; Lord/Lady; Master/slave; Dom/sub; Owner/pet; Daddy/little, etc)

- Psychological dynamics (power exchange; authority transfer, hypnosis, etc)
- Sexual intercourse techniques (I'll leave this one to your imagination)

In BDSM play, one partner may take 30 minutes or more to beautifully and artistically bind their partner in elaborate rope designs and leave them suspended a few feet off the ground; there will only be sex if it had been negotiated previously.

In BDSM play, you may find a couple dressed in some fetish outfit dining at a table set with crystal and bone china. It looks very eccentric, but still a socially acceptable (vanilla) setting. Except that under the table the girl has a bipolar chrome electrical probe inserted into her vagina and her partner is controlling the power box sitting next to his dinner plate. Every so often he turns up the power and she screams. She thinks this is very funny and giggles like mad as soon as she finishes absorbing the intense sensations. This is *good pain*. This is definitely *not* your typical vanilla dinner setting.

BDSM sexual play also differs from vanilla sexual play because the SM activities often act as emotional intensifiers. If you think that the sexual bonding was emotionally spectacular the very first time you had sex, what you will experience with a skilled BDSM practitioner will rock your world. According to the women with whom I've spoken, and according to even a casual Internet search for anecdotal comments, for most women, their first experience blasting off into subspace leaves them astonished and addicted to sensations that are utterly new/foreign to them.

By the way, BDSM and vanilla pairings also differ at the *relationship* level: the BDSM relationship, itself, is often structured to pervade all aspects of the s-type's life—but we'll be covering this a bit further on.

Now—I'm about to wander into the realm of generalities for the remainder of this section. At least I let you know.

Power-neutral relationships

Husband/wife or **boyfriend/girlfriend:** In modern times, men and women strive to show respect for one another by maintaining what we can call *power-equal* relationships. The man may help around the house, he may do some of the grocery shopping; he involves his partner with major decisions. In a general sense, this describes a modern marriage and is often echoed in established boyfriend/girlfriend relationships.

Top/bottom relationships: In BDSM play, the word *Top* (usually capitalized) and the word *bottom* (left in lowercase) merely describe who is *doing* or *receiving* the action. The Top *does things* to the bottom. *Top* and *bottom* describe physical actions and are completely separate from descriptions of the power-based roles such as dominant or submissive. You can be a dominant or a submissive person serving as a Top to flog someone, or you can be a dominant or a submissive person serving as a bottom in order to enjoy a flogging.

When a submissive bottom directs a dominant Top by telling them what to do, this is called *topping from the bottom* and is frowned upon. A person who does this is sometimes called a *smart-assed masochist,* or SAM. You're not going to want to earn that label. Not good. Experienced Tops won't play with you—I've heard of cases where the Top has stopped a scene because the bottom tried to direct the action.

Power-imbalanced relationships

Speaking generally, structured relationships come in two flavors:
- Power-imbalanced relationships (often referred to as D/s)
- Authority-imbalanced relationships (often referred to as M/s for Master/slave, O/p for Owner/property, or TPE for Total Power Exchange)

Despite the BDSM sense that D/s play is time-limited, one also sees long-lasting relationships that have grown to incorporate negotiated D/s into a marriage or marriage-like relationship. In fact, many see power exchange relationships as an effective way that two or more people can choose well-defined roles for themselves and their partner(s). There is a dominant partner who has leadership responsibility and there is a submissive partner (or two) whose responsibilities include both preserving harmony and supporting the dominant. The two (or more) work out ways that their individual abilities can best meet their common needs. There is generally more leeway, more give-and-take in D/s than in M/s structures.

There are a number of common elements between D/s and M/s relationships, and because of that it can be hard to tell them apart. Often, you'll have to ask the D-type how they refer to their particular structure.

Characteristics shared both by D/s and M/s relationships:
- The roles of each partner have been pre-negotiated and there is an agreed-upon leader and follower.
- Most of the relationship parameters have been pre-negotiated and there are stated rules of behavior.
- There are consequences within the relationship for failure to comply with those rules.
- The s-type serves the wants and needs of the D-type.
- The s-type isn't supposed to go off *doing things* without first checking with the D-type.
- The D-type must exhibit above-average ethical and leadership behaviors so the s-type will continue to serve.

Characteristics more common in D/s structures:
- The s-type maintains personal authority over some areas of their life, such as work, biological family, religion, and possibly the time they may spend on their own or doing something they (personally) want to do. They have discussed it and the D-type has agreed to it.
- The s-type retains personal property and control of their own finances.
- Dominance is a key characteristic of the relationship.
- Amorous love (Eros) and friendship (Philos) are more of the focus than spiritual love (Agape)
- Master Skip Chasey refers to D/s as *about the mental body*.

Characteristics more common in M/s structures:
- In part due to their complexity (and in part due to the customs established decades ago within the gay Leather

community) M/s structures often involve a written contract that defines the terms of the *offer* and *acceptance*.

- Master is 100% responsible for all aspects of the slave's well-being—mental health, physical health, finances, etc.
- The emphasis in the relationship is on *growth*. Master is either *growing a slave or growing a man* to use Master Skip Chasey's phrasing in the book edited by david stein titled: *Ask the Man Who Owns Him*.
- Psychological dominance is not a requirement; ethical leadership is a requirement.
- Spiritual love (Agape) and friendship (Philos) are more of the focus than amorous love (Eros).
- M/s relationships often involve a written code of personal and household protocols that describe the way the slave is to behave and the way the household is to run.
- The D-type owns the s-type's time and has been given authority by the s-type to determine the s-type's future.
- The s-type in an M/s relationship is really the Master's/Owner's outreach or advance-man and is expected to know how to react as Master would and to prepare any setting to be exactly as Master wishes it. The s-type is expected to know the D-type as well or better than the D-type knows him/herself.
- The s-type has transferred authority over itself to the D-type: the s-type can no longer refuse an ethical request by the D-type without risking the D-type terminating the entire relationship.
- The s-type has no individual property or money: it all belongs to the D-type.
- Most M/s structures stress the ethical code expressed as HILT: honor, integrity, loyalty, and trust. Words such as focus, purpose, and intent are common M/s topics.
- Master Skip Chasey refers to M/s as *about the spiritual body*. For the many of us who use the M/s dynamic for spiritual connection, the greatest challenge for the slave is what is called *ego surrender* (See: Raven Kalders's book *Sacred Power* for more on this topic). Please refer to the Supplement for resources to help you further explore this area. This is advanced material and not appropriate for this book.

- M/s practitioners often refer to their relationship as a *Family* and often have extended Family members who are part of the House.

While one can make some general observations—as I've just done – the reality is that few authority-imbalanced relationships look alike. This is a prime example of an area where individual needs, preferences, and dreams create the details of an M/s couple's interaction. This is an area where leadership styles, teaching/learning styles, and personal preferences cause relationships to look different to outsiders even when the couple self-identifies in a certain way. When it comes to demonstrating *structure* in relationships, you can have a dozen or so couples that say that they live in a D/s, M/s, O/p, TPE kind of relationship yet appear to outsiders to behave somewhat to very differently. (O/p = Owner/property; TPE = Total Power Exchange)

As you learn more about BDSM relationships, you will learn that these can be very, very sophisticated structures in which the Master is serving the slave's needs every bit as much as the slave is fulfilling Master's wants. To paraphrase Master Ron K in his essay: "On Becoming More…" in Raven Kaldera's book *Sacred Power*, "I am as Master needs, Master is as I desire."

Polyamorous relationships

Polyamory (many loves) is having multiple emotion-based and/or sex-based relationships gong on at one time. Books are filled with discussions about monogamy and polyamory. In the simplest way, some who practice BDSM remain monogamous and some don't. As with all relationships, these decisions evolve from the needs/wants of each couple. Of the many varieties of non-monogamous relationships, most fall into one of two categories: *open* sex-based relationships and *polyamorous structures* that may or may not include sex.

(Note: polyamory does not equate to *swinging*: they are emotional opposites. Swinging is designed to be *No-Strings-Attached* (NSA) sex. Polyamory is designed to be shared emotional connections with others where *sex* is a separate discussion/negotiation that is certainly not assumed.)

Open relationships themselves fall generally into two camps: those that permit outside casual NSA sex, and those that permit their partner to maintain one or more emotionally connected partners. This latter form is sometimes referred to as a polyamorous V structure. In this structure, while one person has two (or more) emotionally-connected relationships (that may or may not include sex), the people who are sharing this one person may not, themselves, have any kind of personal relationship.

Polyamory comes into play when both partners in a committed relationship accept a third (or fourth or fifth…) into their lives—usually but not necessarily including sex.

Sado-masochistic roles

Sadomasochism is a word from psychology used to describe sexual practices characterized both by sadism and masochism. Sadism and masochism are emotionally loaded terms in Western culture. Normally, if you say that someone is a sadist you mean that the person enjoys being cruel or doing cruel things to people. In English, nothing good comes to mind when you hear someone described as a sadist. Interestingly, nothing good comes to mind when you hear someone described as a masochist, either. Just think: a masochist evokes the image of someone who does things the hard way or sacrifices himself or herself for others (for example, someone who constantly works overtime despite their protestations about how they deplore doing so).

As I mention in the glossary (see Supplement A), a **sadist** in the context of BDSM is a person who receives (erotic) pleasure from *giving others* strong sensations that may temporarily include moderate to severe pain or suffering, and a **masochist** is the opposite—a person who feels (erotic) pleasure from *receiving* strong sensations that may temporarily include moderate to severe pain or suffering. Before you balk too much at that description, consider this: the person receiving the intense sensations has eroticized them. They may have started their BDSM path saying *ouch*, but now they say *ahhhhhhh!*. Actually, one of the many confusing aspects of BDSM is that some people *enjoy* being hurt/punished and seek relationships based on *domestic discipline* and related non-erotic pain-based activities.

Obviously, one's interest in giving or receiving intense sensations is a sliding scale. Some bottoms agree to receive intense stimulation as a way of demonstrating love and obedience to their partner while others personally enjoy and benefit directly from receiving intense stimulations. Psychologically, the difference is that the former are looking *outward* from themselves to the relationship and accepting often-painful stimulation as one aspect of bonding with their partner, while the latter are looking *inward* and feeding off of the pain for their own erotic purposes. There is a big difference between these two, and this is important knowledge to have, for within a relationship it speaks to a partner's *motivation* in wanting to receive stimulation.

In the same way I've described the sliding scale of interest that a bottom has for receiving intense stimulation, there is a similar sliding scale of interest that a Top has for administering it. At one end, you'll find sadistic Tops who derive personal gratification from the SM play, itself, while at the other end you'll find service Tops whose pleasure comes from pleasing another person by providing the painful sensations being requested (while also engaged in an activity that they enjoy). In the first case, it is *the SM play* that the Top is enjoying, in the second case, it is *the opportunity to please another person* that the Top is enjoying. Again, this boils down to a case of a person's *outward* or *inward* focus. By the way, many Tops are willing to act as service Tops in order to help friends or newcomers explore new activities. In this case, the Top is just being friendly and helpful and falls in the dead center of that figurative sliding scale.

Now that you have that general background, here is more detail:

Sadists
In the world of BDSM, the line between pathological sadism and a sadistic play style is enforced through negotiated consent. That is, if the bottom consents to the Top's physical or emotional acts of sadism, then the relationship is deemed to fall under SSC (Safe, Sane, and Consensual) rules and will be accepted by the community. (Remember:

Generalizations about Sado-masochistic Roles in the BDSM Culture

A sadistic BDSM player plays for their own pleasure
and enjoys watching the bottom's discomfort and pain.

A sensory sadist derives pleasure from giving intense
sensations other than pain
(think about tickle-torture, ice dildos, forced orgasms).

A sensual sadist enjoys giving intense sensations,
including sexual and erotic sensations that might include
severe pain,
but with great consideration for the bottom's pleasure.

A service Tops' pleasure comes from using SM skills to please
another person
while engaged in an activity that they enjoy.

Sometimes, a Top will act as a service Top
in order to help a friend or newcomer explore a new activity.

masochistic and sadistic behaviors are not related to power dynamics. A dominant, submissive, or switch can be a masochist, a sadist, or none of the above.)

Researchers have four general classifications of sexual sadist:
- Class I: those who are bothered by their sadistic fantasies but don't act on them.
- Class II: those who act on their sadistic sexual urges with consenting partners who willingly suffer pain or humiliation. (At one end of the spectrum, their partners may be sexual masochists who really enjoy the pain; at the other end of that

spectrum are people with various self-image issues that see the humiliation as affirmation of their worthlessness.)
- Class III: sadists who act on their sadistic sexual urges with non-consenting victims but do not seriously injure or kill them. In most states this can lead to legal charges of sexual battery (the terms are state-specific).
- Class IV: sexual sadists who not only act on their sadistic sexual urges with non-consenting victims but also seriously injure or kill them. Class III and class IV sexual sadists are loosely grouped by psychologists as *sexual aggressors*.

Sadists within the BDSM world fall predominantly into Classes I and II with a very few Class III cases cropping up every so often. Real sadists—Classes III and IV—aren't as likely to reveal themselves within a BDSM club/group setting, as they quickly get into trouble with play partners and get banished. Gossip about a bad sadistic scene will tear through a community's submissives' network like a straw house catching fire.

Masochists
For BDSMers, there is a psychological safety issue concerning masochistic submissives. A person with low self-esteem entering the BDSM community tends to do what people tell them to do: their *self-preservation* wiring is not connected correctly. Since they often feel that they deserve to be hurt, they get into situations where they get hurt: this can be a recipe for abuse. On the other hand, if a person enters this community with a good sense of self, a clear understanding of the ethics and leadership they seek in a partner, and—by the way—enjoy erotic pain, that's a whole different story.

In the same way that some people like steak and potatoes and other people like liver and onions, people who like pain have different reasons for liking it. The best categorization I have ever seen of different motivations people have for enjoying pain was created by Maître Pierre and Mistress Catharine (owners of www.BDSMCircle.net). They have graciously given me permission to reprint their list. Should you wish to read more high-quality material from them, their weblink is: www.bdsmcircle.net/dslifestyle/paininbdsm.htm.

"The context BDSM masochist: For them, pain is not important. Actually, many of them have no pain tolerance whatsoever. For them, the excitement comes from the surrounding, the context of the scene, the SM toys, the dungeon. A well-equipped dungeon is the top pleasure for them. To satisfy them, the key word is *diversity*. They get tired quickly of the same thing. They want more SM toys used on them; they want more sensations. The trick with them is to keep an ace up your sleeve; don't reveal everything to them. When they get bored, these types of players often simply look for another Dominant to find something new, so these players tend not to be faithful to their Dominants.

"The endorphin BDSM masochist: The key word here *endorphin*! This type of BDSM masochist is into pain in order to get the euphoric endorphin effects. Often, they will accept a Master/slave structure on the condition that their partner can provide that endorphin fix. Most of these BDSM masochists can be very tough and can take a substantial amount of pain, toughness they got from lots of SM play. they will be very faithful to their partner (either D- or s-type) so long as this person can give them the pain they want and need.

"The exhibitionist BDSM masochist: Appearances are everything! To be seen, the most beautiful equipment, the one that takes the most pain, the most beautiful clothing. Being the center of attention is what is important. For this type of BDSM masochist (the *stand-and-model* form of SM), there isn't a lot of interest in having a private scene, but being in a public BDSM setting is very important for them.

"The sexual BDSM masochist: The BDSM scene is the context to receive sexual pain. For women this can include fisting, various kind of insertions, and even rape simulations. For men this can include anal fisting, sodomy, and rape simulations. Strangely enough, men in this category often like sexual orgasm control because of its physical effects! This type of BDSM masochist may not prove to be faithful to their Master (Mistress); their needs may drive them to seek new sensation from somebody other than their usual partner."

As you read that list, you may feel that you are a blend of more than one category of masochist. This is understandable, as we're not made from cookie-cutter molds. I've included this list for two reasons. First, Maître Pierre and Mistress Catharine point out that it can help Dom/mes to know how to create a good BDSM scene that is adapted to the submissive's style if they can figure out where a submissive falls within this classification. Second, I thought this categorization was well thought out and congruent with my own experience of our BDSM community.

Chapter 5
Negotiations, Contracts and Collars

Negotiations, contracts, collars and protocol manuals are generally the domain of Master/slave relationship structures. In fact, I developed the material in this chapter for my book titled: *Master/slave Mastery: Updated handbook of concepts, approaches, and practices,* but decided to modify it to fit a D/s relationship and include it here.

I suspect that for those still fairly new to BDSM the idea of negotiating the *relationship* in addition to negotiating a *scene* may cause some to through up their hands up in frustration over the amount of work that this culture involves.

Take heart…

It's for your own good.

Let me explain.

In the same way that *negotiating the terms and parameters of a scene* helps to ensure that both parties' needs are met and that you have a successful outcome, the same applies even more strongly to your relationship.

Think about it: you're both grown-ups. You both have been places and done things and formed opinions about who you are and who you want to be. Importantly, you've formed some opinions about who you want to live with. Some serious talking about your impending relationship is bound to help, yes?

I'd like to make a proposal to you: I propose that if you'll go through the time and trouble to prepare at least a contract tied to collaring stages, you'll have a better time if it with your partner than if you give in to lust and just move in together.

Why? Because if the two (or more) of you actually sit down and discuss your wants and needs and how each of you can help the other fulfill their dreams, our chances of success have just gone up substantially: You replace *chance* with *planning*—resulting in focused intent: always a good thing.

About Thinking

"It's not *what* you think about the relationship, it's *how* you think about the relationship."

—Master Jim Glass, Northeast Master/slave Conference, 2006

In life, one gets what one asks for. Structured relationships—regardless of the degree of control that one partner has over the other—differ from vanilla relationships: you get the opportunity to negotiate what you want from your partner before you declare the relationship to exist and invest emotionally in its success. Unlike most vanilla boyfriend/girlfriend structures where each person has beliefs and expectations about the other person's probable behavior, those starting a Dominant/submissive structure have quite a bit to discuss before making it public.

Contracts are not created BY the D-type and summarily offered TO the s-type. When developed together, they go a long way towards uncovering strong personal preferences that hadn't come up yet in your discussions—because your discussions have largely been focused on learning about BDSM and SM play techniques. Interestingly, the more prior relationships you've had—particularly long relationships or marriages—the more useful a contract can be.

You're more aware of what went wrong before that you could avoid this time. Consider it to be a kinky pre-nuptial agreement that lays out zones of authority and responsibility.

In Master/slave structured relationships, there commonly are two types of documents, a Contract and a Protocol Manual. These are parallel to a corporation's Articles of Incorporation and By-Laws: in our form of government, they are parallel to the Constitution and the Bill of Rights. However, formal protocols (a written document prepared by the D-type and inform the s-type of how things are to be done) are not very common in Dominant/submissive relationships, so I won't discuss protocols in this book.

(Note: See Supplement B for recommended books on protocols. If you're envisioning your relationship to be so deep and committed that your *relationship*, itself, becomes the focus of your kink (rather than SM play), then I urge you to learn more about the worlds of Masters and slaves. It's different. Very different.)

However, at *this* stage—at the stage where you are newish to BDSM, it makes sense to have some serious discussions about what each of you are hoping to achieve by hooking up. It' better than guessing.

Oh—and contracts come in different flavors.
- They come in the *scene contract* flavor that is pretty straightforward (This is what we've agreed to do, right? Please sign here.)
- They come in the *training contract* flavor (Okay, we're going to give this a shot for three months: this is what I intend to do with you and this is what I expect you to do during this period, right? Please sign here.)
- And, they come in the *permanent collar* variety (I hereby take you under these terms and conditions until one of us violates the trust of the other; you agree to serve and obey me, right? Please sign here.)

Thinking about negotiations

Contracts result from negotiations. They are not pulled off the Web; they are not borrowed from Dom/me X down the street. Contracts give the D-type the opportunity to say: "Look, this is what I believe in, this is what I'm concerned about, this is how I'd like you to interact with me... now tell me what you believe in and whether anything in here might not feel right for you." Contracts give the s-type the opportunity to say: "Well, this is okay, but can we phrase this a little differently, and oh-by-the-way, my ex-husband used to want me to do that and it became a real sore point, so you may as well forget it right now."

For contracts to work, they must be real.

For the initial training contract to work, it has to be fairly simple and non-threatening.

Note to D-types: This person may not know you very well (or be much junior to you in the lifestyle), so the very fact that you're presenting them with a contract may be intimidating. The longer and more complex the contract, the more likely they'll be cautious about it. Use the KISS approach: *Keep It Simple, Stupid.*

For many of us in this community, *ownership* is the dividing line between being a Dom/me and being a Master/Owner: it's also a key difference between being a submissive and being a slave. Said differently, while a Dom/me has **influence** over their submissive, a Master has **authority** over their slave. (This is why one refers to a D/s structure is based in *power exchange* and is generally scene-specific, while one refers to am M/s structure as *authority transfer* and represents an ongoing commitment.)

The D/s and M/s labels are often used differently by different couples. Some D/s structures may appear to be acting like an M/s structure and many M/s structures may appear to be acting more like a D/s structure. It's hard to tell from the outside. Because of that, I've included this material on negotiations, contracts, and collars. This gives you *information*—what you do with it is wholly up to you.

If you've not done a fair amount of negotiation in your life, you'll want to read these sections more than once. Also, if you're negotiating with an intended s-type who has not negotiated a number of prior contracts, moral/ethical honor binds you to recommend to your intended that he/she seek an experienced D-type to represent him/her in negotiations with YOU.

Opening Notes: In real-life business negotiations, it is a truism that the *real guts of the negotiation occur just as the clock is running out.* That is, if you allow an hour for a negotiation, most of the serious issues get negotiated in the last five minutes. If you allow a day, they get negotiated in the last five minutes. If you allow a week, they get negotiated in the last five minutes.

Also, you will be able to conclude a much more successful negotiation if you understand your s-type's needs/wants through their eyes. The better you understand what the *other person* **needs** vs. **wants**, the cleaner and clearer the negotiation. That said, I'll now start in on this section.

≠≠≠≠≠≠≠≠≠≠≠≠≠≠≠≠≠≠≠≠≠≠≠≠≠≠≠≠≠≠≠

Negotiation rules

You might think that you can sit right down and negotiate what you want/need from this relationship, yes? Without any prep, yes?

Ah, that would be a "No."

Not unless you're prepared to take the smaller portion. Here are some general observations and rules about negotiating:
- We negotiate all the time.
- Almost everything is negotiable.
- Avoid taking a position early in the discussion.
- First, figure out how to create value. Why should someone want *you* or what you are offering?
- Why *didn't* this person's last partner want them?
- The first option isn't necessarily the best. Create many options.

- Deadlines can be tricky when you're negotiating matters of the heart. (The general rule in business negotiations is to negotiate early or risk your opponent using deadlines—real or imagined—to trap you into conceding in their favor.)
- Use: "What if..." questions to break open the discussion to create value.
- You must leave the other person with a sense of satisfaction. This is the *win/win* school of negotiation, not the *winner takes all* school.
- Do your homework. Try to figure out what your partner needs that they aren't telling you outright. Determine *why* your intended partner is seeking certain specific terms or conditions.
- Use imaginative language to take the other person into the future to see possible results of various roles.

Actually, there are a couple of "rules" that can keep you out of most difficulties:

- Rule One: Particularly with new play partners, begin your negotiations by eMail so you have a paper trail. This avoids "he said/she said" fights.
- Rule Two: Negotiate only what you **will permit**: don't try to list everything you **won't** permit. Reason: the list of what you *will* permit is fairly limited—after all, you only have a set amount of time. However, you're not likely to think of all the things you *won't* permit, and the top can argue that since you didn't specifically exclude some form of play it is technically not on your "red" list.

WHAT to negotiate?

When you're reading this material, please keep in mind that you're probably going to start out with a *training contract*, and not a full-blown D/s or M/s contract—for those are hugely different. This is the *getting-to-know-you* stage, not the *okay, here we go* stage. So: you'll have to pick and choose from among these points to create contract that meets your particular needs.

In a general way, I suggest you negotiate the *indicators of success for the next three months.* What does *success* look like to Master and to slave? What does *failure* look like?

[Note: the points I listed here live outside the boilerplate language of a contract. I'll assume that D-type is agreeing to cherish and to train s-type in various ways; I'll assume that s-type is agreeing to serve with humility and to please D-type in various ways, and so forth. These comments go beyond those statements/actions.]

- If you're going to require the s-type to be studying, how much time does that involve per day or week?
- If the slave is going to be journaling, what is the content of the entries and how long must they be? (NOTE: I failed to negotiate this with my slave, and, as a result, she thought that sending me summaries of her day fulfilled her journaling obligations. I was looking for introspection and didn't care very much about what she did at work during the day. As a result, we were both disappointed about the journaling experience: she was hurt that I didn't respond to her writing; I was disappointed that I wasn't getting much substance out of the exercise.)
- If you are going to allow your s-type to retain certain rights, be crystal clear about that. For example, at this early stage, will D-type have authority over the s-type's...
  - Contact with their family and friends?
  - Use of money, including clothing purchases?
  - Hair/makeup style?
  - Workplace and work hours?
  - Weight and food choices?
- During this trial period, you may want a monogamous relationship. But, there are many combinations out there. I know of a case where the D-type wanted to take the s-type to swingers parties: that has to be negotiated up front. I know another case where a woman had her own vanilla lover of many years before becoming an s-type to another man. These special situations have to be addressed with care and sensitivity.

- Staying on the sexual front for a minute, will you, as the D-type, require the s-type to stop all self-pleasuring during this period? And what if the D-type considers eating chocolate to be a good example of self-pleasuring? Again, be specific.
- How much responsibility is the D-type agreeing to take on during this opening period? What if...
   o The s-type is fired from work five weeks into the relationship and can't make their rent payment? Do you take over?
   o The s-type is out running an errand for you and is injured in a car accident; what is your moral/ethical position? What if it's YOUR car?
   o You are playing with your s-type and you hit a *land mine* that triggers a psychotic episode; he/she requires long-term therapy. What's your moral/ethical position in *this* case?
- If you wish your s-type to dress in a certain way, who's paying for the outfits during the trial period? Will you pay for the first $500 for outfits that please you? The first $200 or $1,500? (You may think I'm pulling this stuff out of thin air—I'm not. My fetish involves dressing elaborately for full fetish formal dinners. We do this many times a week. For me, my partner's appeal is affected by how she looks when *all dressed up.* Dressing this way extends to manicures, pedicures, and shoe choice, as well as hair and makeup combinations. The question now becomes: *What will you pay—in time and money—to make your relationship magical?*)
- If you are requiring a *full disclosure contract*, does your s-type candidate fully understand exactly what you mean by that phrase? You may want to explain clearly that this will mean that you can rightfully demand to know from your s-type *anything* that another person says to them in confidence. Further, you should explain that your s-type will be bound to volunteer that information to you if, in their heart-of-hearts, they know that you really should know about it. Jay Wiseman points out that this creates a separate duty on the s-type's part to tell someone *in advance* that nothing said to this slave can be held in confidence.

Too much work? Think you can bypass some of this minutiae? Maybe, maybe not. Did you ever consider what could happen if you *don't* go through a thorough negotiation process? Seen this one, lately? It's called *The Etiology of a Crisis*. I've added the M/s storyline.

- **Wild Enthusiasm:** Ohmygosh, I finally found someone willing to be my slave!!
- **Disillusionment:** Ohmygosh, this person is not such a good fit; how could I have done this???
- **Total Confusion:** Ohmygosh, I actually signed a three-month training contract with this person, and my word is my bond, and he/she's making me crazy.
- **Search for the Guilty:** This must be their fault. They must have hidden faults from me—everyone knows I'm an excellent judge of people.
- **Punishment of the Innocent:** Okay, I'll terminate our contract on the grounds that they won't obey me and then make up some reason why I can excuse myself for treating them as my enemy within the Community.
- **Promotion of the Uninvolved:** I'll go over here and take X as my new slave. This will show everyone who is watching that there's nothing wrong with ME.

Problems with Negotiations— YOU as the Buyer

Some negotiations go better than others, yes? Sometimes you come away feeling really good about the outcome, but sometimes you feel that the other person got more than you did. Here are some reasons.

Disparity of power

- You may be exhibiting—or you may be negotiating with someone exhibiting—*Alpha male* characteristics—pushy and assertive/aggressive. Apart from having to decide if you want this kind of personality in your life, you may find it nearly impossible to be *heard*. That's a problem.
- Your opposite (either the D-type looking for the s-type or the s-type looking for the D-type) may need to sell themselves to you more than you need to add them to your life.

- *Disparity of information*
- Your opposite may have done much more research on you than you did on him/her.
- Your opposite may be *much more experienced* in D/s (or M/s) relations than you, and may **assume** that you know/ understand things that never even occurred to you.
- The other person may specifically be *hiding things from you.*
- Your opposite may know that he/she has another candidate in the wings if you don't work out. In the alternative, they may know YOU have another candidate waiting, if they don't work out.

Disparity of experience
- You may have this kind of interview/negotiation all the time; your opposite may do it only once or twice a year. This is particularly true of DomSMes who may be (culturally) more used to being the negotiators in relationships, and also of Dom/mes who may be more used to interviewing or negotiating with subs for BDSM scenes or for relationship positions.
- Your s-type candidate may not be used to thinking like a salesman—yet the success of this negotiation depends upon each of your selling points.

Disparity of pressure
- Is your opposite a high-value D- or s-type? That is, if you don't compromise and agree to their terms, are there likely to be other people waiting to accept those terms?
- Are you rushing in to replace a relationship that just ended? Are you under social or personal pressure to demonstrate that you're okay and the proof is that you can immediately form another relationship?

Hmmm. Lots to think about.

Let me offer a quick recap. You're serious about starting a new relationship. You've decided that this potential partner is okay—no skeletons hiding in the closet—you've read about negotiations, and you're ready to put your first contract together.

Good going. You're right in here with me.

Contracts

I've heard people dismiss M/s contracts out-of-hand. Their argument is that because it's not possible to make a legally binding contract in the U.S. that gives enforceable control over one person to another person that therefore there is no point to it—that it is a waste of time.

I differ.

Strongly.

While contracts have no standing in court, the very process of writing a contract forces the two of you to talk about and work through the most fundamental aspects of your proposed lives together. Even if you're both married to one another and are now converting your marriage to D/s or M/s, the contracting phases enables the two (or more) parties to sit down and work through relationship issues that are often *assumed* to be one way or another.

Contracts become a way of making a record of what each of you were thinking (hoping for) when you started your relationship. People tend to forget things; details wash away with time—and age. Contracts don't change their minds. This is not a trivial issue. A clearly worded contract helps prevent needless upsets and recriminations...
    "But you promised me..."
    "I never said any such thing..."
    "But I thought you meant..."
    "You never asked..."

Contracts also can serve as a way to put boundaries around the initial emotions-gone-wild initial months of a new relationship. In fact, I'd personally suggest that initial contract shouldn't be more than 3-6 months long in order to see yourselves safely through the *lust* phase and into the *logic* phase. In a way, contracts force people to bring up tough topics, topics often glossed over. In that light, contracts serve to protect people who don't know one another very well but who want to trust and want to do really risky things. This contracting process helps to balance the physically kinky risks by anchoring the emotional risks.

Contracts are really enabling each person to say: "This is what I'm offering and this is what I hope to get out of it; what are *you* offering and what do *you* want to get out of this? Beyond the sex, why is *living with me* appealing for you?"

You'll understand how contracts can be simplified once you gain experience in these kinds of relationships. For those still relatively new, though, they are a very effective way to get to know more about how your prospective partner thinks and what, exactly, they think their roles are going to be.

Finally, there's a subtle and very important reason that a D-type would prepare a contract for the s-type: contracts serve to stabilize the emotional side of a relationship in order that the submissive is more able to offer their body for some risky SM play. That is—by talking through the *relationship* part of equation, the s-type is much more likely to be willing to risk a bit more with the physical side of the equation.

So: contracts are serious pledges—and one of their characteristics is that there is an end-date. Contracts expire. This can be a good thing, though, for the end of one contract period presents an opportunity for each of you to modify aspects of the contract that didn't work so well before you sign up for another contract period.

Here's a tip: There's an advantage to building a contract-review process into whatever contract you end up writing. I'd recommend that you include a provision to enable both of you to come back to being of equal negotiating power in order to be able to say such things as: "Some of my relationship needs have changed and I'm not sure you've realized these changes have occurred." *Changes* can be physical or mental.

In this book, I've included three sample contracts: a training contract, a very detailed long-term contract, and a very short *Owner's contract*. However, before you start reading those, I'd still like to discuss some of the common styles of contracts and some of the more common clauses in contracts of this kind. By now, you probably have one eyebrow cocked and are reflecting on my opening aphorism: *When you don't know what to do, do it slowly.* Yes, this entire process takes a while.

Styles of Contracts

So, let's say you are, in fact, going to prepare a document that specifies the contractual obligations of the partners, better to understand the proposed power exchange relationship. There are three main ways to consider doing this that have worked for other people. I'm sure that there are other ways to do it, but these are the more common ways of approaching contracts in the BDSM world.

- **Time-controlled contract:** This defines the obligations and duties each will assume at certain points along their agreed path. Normally, the defined level of power exchange starts as a simple structured definition of the relationship at the time. The contract specifies the **furthest** level of power exchange that is comfortable for both parties and explains commensurate duties and obligations. In between are a number of stages, normally between two and four, with each step mapped out.

  The level of power exchange is normally increased over time, though I am aware of one where the final stage was a required dissolution of the relationship. The timing of when the contractual stages come into force are not usually in the contract. Instead, it is up to the s-type to inform the D-type that he/she is ready for the next stage (thus giving consent), and for the D-type then to inform the s-type when the next stage will come into effect (thus retaining control).

  This type of contract may be most applicable when two people are quite certain at the outset that their relationship will work out, and they know the path along which they wish to travel. While I've never known a couple to use this structure, it seems to me that this would be useful when the D-type is much more experienced than s-type and is clear about where they wish to lead that s-type over time.

- **Several contracts used in stages:** This type of contract may be more applicable when two people wish to begin exploring a path together. Here, the D-type may begin with some kind of temporary contract—perhaps a contract that covers a weekend, or a week or so. This can be viewed as a *getting to know you* kind of contract. It may be fairly brief, but it gives each partner some starting points for developing their relationship.

  Next, the D-type may offer a training contract that could last for a number of months, and could, perhaps, be renewed if the D-type didn't feel the slave had accomplished enough during the first contract period.

  Following that, the D-type may offer a more extensive contract during a courting period—a period where he/she is deciding whether to accept this s-type for a lifetime commitment.

  Finally, the D-type may offer the s-type a much simplified contract for life.

  Some notes:
  - o Each time one contract ends, the NEXT contract is negotiated and prepared. This is done so that both parties understand the level of power exchange they must now meet, and also (as with the single time-controlled contract) understand the objective for the next stage, so they can strive to meet it.
  - o A new *type* of contract is only created once the D-type is assured that the intent of the previous contract has been fulfilled; that the s-type has been able to live within the power and authority structure described in the expiring contract.
  - o Although it may be hard to accomplish, I strongly suggest that you let one contract expire and use the next 4-6 weeks to negotiate the next staged contract from a position of *equal personal power*. That is, I

urge you NOT to negotiate the next contract from within the D/s or M/s relationship. This is particularly important in cases where the s-type has given their personal authority to the D-type for the last number of months: how in the world does he/she suddenly have the power to *negotiate?*

- **Single stage (simple) contract**: This contract lays out the core obligations and duties on both sides. This defines the balance of power or authority exchange at the time and leaves open any decrease or increase in that exchange. Typically, these contracts have no ending date. This contract is also known as a No Limits Contract and is sometimes seen in an Owner/slave relationship, rather than a Master/slave relationship. Often, the exchange is thus:
  o D-type agrees to cherish and care for the s-type and always to work for the their physical, mental, emotional, social, spiritual, and financial wellbeing.
  o s-type agrees to serve and to obey the D-type.

Common Wording in Contracts

A cautionary beginning: When I started reviewing online slave contracts, I was be struck by (actually, appalled by) the language giving the Master permission to punish and control the slave. In my experience, those who have chosen the path of *slave* view it as a *calling.* They are seeking to be recognized and cherished for doing a good job in their service—and *punishment* for trivial issues will drive them from the relationship.

NOTE: I realize that *domestic discipline* is a fetish and that some (bratty?) s-types are seeking a strong D-type specifically to be caught and punished at every opportunity. That form of relationship is different from the kinds of relationships that I'm describing in this book. There is nothing wrong with domestic discipline fetishes so long as both partners think it's a lot of fun. The real risk takes the form of the potential that the D-type's discipline has a negative effect on the s-type's self-image.

Along this same line, I strongly urge you to consider that many of the slave contracts you'll find online stem from the porn version of Masters and slaves. In real life, whether M/s or D/s, you have a leader and a follower and each of you are trying to get clear about what the other expects so you won't be bumping in power shields.

There are many sample contracts available on the Internet. You may find it hard to identify a pre-existing contract that you could use—without alteration—in your own real-life relationship. That's because people (and their relationships) are so different. At any rate, when drawing up a personal contact, you might want to consider:

- **Key actors:** Who are each of you? What roles do you intend to play?
- **Exclusivity:** Are both of you single and unattached or are others to be involved in this relationship? If *others,* then go into detail describing everyone's role and responsibility.
- **Biological Family:** What provisions are made for any biological family members, especially minor children or aged parents?
- **Breadth of control:** Does this contract hold true outside the house or only at home? If it carries outside the house, where should you both agree that there are exceptions to the control agreed upon in this contract?
  - s-type's biological family
  - Professional/work life
  - Religious/spiritual training
  - Existing financial condition—savings/retirement accounts, future earnings, etc.
- **Outedness:** (I know it's not a word.) Are either of you *out* or still closeted? Will either of you be using a scene name? Does your biological family know about your lifestyle and relationship choices? How will you behave in public? How are you going to behave at your family's Holiday party?
- **Health:** Here, discuss issues of fluid bonding, sexually transmitted infections, safer-sex practices, and any mental health issues you know of. [NOTE: I recommend that you do NOT include any specific discussion of weight loss or exercise in your contract. However, you *can* mutually commit to the

concept of maintaining some mutually agreed-upon fitness standard. It makes much more sense for specific exercise requirements to be part of your Protocol Manual. Also, dietary and exercise requirements may change over time, but the Contract does *not* change over time.]

- **Mutual wants and needs:** Simply put—what does each party to this contract get out of signing it? What is the benefit to the D- and s-type? Will the s-type agree to cosmetic surgery? Will the s-type agree to specialized training, such as attending a cooking or butlering academy? Might the s-type be required to learn another language or move out of the US? Will the D-type go through management or team training courses? Will the D-type study communication and teaching strategies?

- **Property:** May the s-type own property? May they bring property with them into the relationship? As previously mentioned… who owns the s-type's current assets and debts? Will finances now be shared or kept separate?

- **Speaking freely:** will the s-type be permitted to speak freely to the D-type? If yes, are there protocols that shield the s-type from being punished for speaking freely? Does this contract recognize that the s-type is honor-bound to notify the D-type when the D-type is about to do something that is seriously not-okay with the s-type? Does this contract include provisions for slave to alert the D-type to some serious issue/problem when in public without violating the authority imbalance? (This kind of material is covered in detail in my *Protocols* book.)

- **Punishment:** Will you distinguish between *punishment* and *correction*? Do you distinguish between *punishment* and *funishment*? Will you distinguish between *reactance* and *resistance*? Under what circumstances may the D-type punish the s-type? What will be involved in that punishment? Will there be release through atonement after the punishment?

- **Safety**: What emotional and financial safeguards are you going to put in place for the s-type, both during the relationship and upon the relationship's end? What physical play safeword will you be using, *Red*? What emotional upset safeword will you be using, the D-type's given name?

- **Sexuality**: Does this contract include sex? If so, how is *sex* defined. Is it *intercourse* or is it *SM play* of some kind? Or something else? Is the D-type free to play sexually with others? Is the s-type equally free to play with others? Can the s-type be loaned out? Will this be a multi-s-type Household? This is the place to discuss any issues of polyamory, swinging, multiple slaves, and so forth. This is also the place to discuss sex with others of the same gender.

- **Openness**: Is the nature of the relationship to be discreet, or open and obvious to the public, work colleagues, family, etc.? Have you discussed *transparency*? Does the D-type recognize his/her own obligation to be transparent to the s-type? Does the s-type realize that the D-type requires transparency in order to make wise and informed decisions about the s-type and the relationship?

- **Discipline**: What is the nature and extent of the D-type's control? How is discipline to be administered? Are there any restrictions on forms of discipline? For example, you may wish not to use any type of BDSM implement that is also used for scening. The issues: implements used for scening carry positive associations and related positive emotions. If you start using the same implement for punishment, you will lose some/most/all of those special and positive associations with that implement. Similarly, if the s-type was punished in a particular way in the past—particularly by parents—that form of punishment may now trigger land mines—you'll want to discuss that in the contract.

- **Finance**: Explain how pre-existing wealth, as well as income subsequent to the contract, is to be handled. For example, during the training contract, you may not wish to address any aspect of your s-type's finances—just mark that section *reserved*. On the other hand, if this is to be a Master/slave contract and your slave candidate is very experienced (has lived as a slave for many years), he/she may expect to surrender personal control over their finances.

- **Duration**: How long is your contract? Under what conditions—and following what procedure—can it be terminated? (Let me pretend we're speaking about an M/s contract for a minute, not a D/s contract. In the M/s world, contract duration is a hotly discussed topic. In the gay community, there is a tendency to spend some time getting to know one another before extending a contract without a termination date—a contract for life. Among the heterosexual M/s movement, there is a much stronger tendency to create a series of staged contracts that carry termination dates. There is also a substantial camp that believes that a contract must have a termination date in order to be realistic, particularly because they recognize that the slave (and even the Master) may change a great deal during this experience, and Master wants to be able to reevaluate the slave every year or so, in light of their experiences together.)

Why is this section so long and complex?

There is no such thing as a standard contract for authority-imbalanced relationships. You're cutting new ground for yourself. You have to tailor this—or any other preexisting contract—to your own situation.

Typical simple contract covering the training period. (Remember: these are sample contracts and are only included as examples, not as models.)

Of my own free will, as of _____(date), I _____(name), hereby grant you,_____(name), full ownership and use of my body and mind from now until _____(date).

I will obey you at all times and will wholeheartedly seek your pleasure and well-being above all other considerations.

I renounce all rights to my own pleasure, comfort, or gratification, except insofar as you desire or permit them.

I will strive diligently to re-mold my body, my habits, and my attitudes in accordance with your desires.

I will seek always to learn how to please you better, and will gracefully accept criticism.

I renounce all rights to privacy or concealment from you. I will answer truthfully and completely, to the best of my knowledge, any and all questions you may ask me.

I understand and agree that any failure by me to comply fully with your desires shall be regarded as sufficient cause for possibly severe punishment.

Within the limits of physical safety and my ability to earn a livelihood, I otherwise unconditionally accept as your prerogative anything you may choose to do with me, whether as punishment, for your amusement, or for whatever purpose, no matter how painful or humiliating to myself.

_____(name)

_____(date)

_____(place)

Suggestions for a Contract beyond the Training Level

There are very few very good Websites that I'd send you to for contracts:

- *Negotiated Boundaries* contract for the enslavement term (*www.asubmissivesjourney.com/contract.html*)
- Best contract I've ever seen—highly recommended *http://everything2.com/title/a+real-life+slave+contract*

A quick word about collars

In the worlds of BDSM, many couples use a **collar**—a band, strip, or chain worn around the neck of the submissive partner—as a symbol of ownership of one partner by another. Someone wearing a collar to symbolize his or her relationship status is said to be *collared*. For some, collaring a submissive or slave is a very private thing, for others it represents an opportunity to publically (and formally) recognize their relationship, much like a marriage ceremony. While you'll see many varieties of collars, perhaps the style most frequently used is a black leather band—often containing a metal D-ring (in order to be able to attach a leash).

The collar clearly belongs to the D-type and is worn by the s-type solely at the D-type's discretion. Should the relationship end, the collar remains with the D-type. Although fairly rare, I know of a number of un-collaring ceremonies where the couple disengages from one another in a public way. In many situations, this actually helps both people re-integrate into their communities as single people without the risk of people trying to guess about why they are no longer a couple.

Collars have varying degrees of significance within the BDSM community. A person wearing a collar may wish to signal that he or she is submissive or may wish to signal that they are *owned* by (or are in a relationship with) a Dom/Master. A lockable collar may further symbolize a transfer of power or authority from the person wearing the collar to the person holding the key. Because an obvious collar would be inappropriate in some business settings, some submissives are permitted to wear their collars only when in private with their partners or with other members of the BDSM community. So if someone is wearing a collar, chances are they are of a submissive persuasion; but not all subs wear collars full time.

To further complicate matters, collars may be used in role-playing games involving D/s play or humiliation play, as they have connotations of control and pet-like status, especially when worn with a leash. Thus, it is possible to see someone you thought was an uncollared submissive wearing a collar in a scene.

As BDSM practices increasingly move into middle class society, the role of the collar has also changed. Increasingly, couples that also practice 24/7 D/s relationships adopt collars that can be mistaken as ordinary chokers or jewelry necklaces and can be worn discreetly in public. In BDSM parlance, such items are often referred to as *everyday collars*.

Stages of collaring

While there is no particular formality or rule about it, some in the BDSM community use three stages of collaring. Under this system, the first collar is termed the *collar of consideration*, the second is termed a *training collar*, and the third is the *permanent collar* or a *slave collar.*

Collar of Consideration: A Collar of Consideration is usually worn for a negotiated period, however either party can remove this collar at any time and for any reason, ending the relationship without ill will or recriminations. If the submissive remains collared through the contracted period, there are then three options: First, the existing relationship status can be extended; second, the relationship can be ended amicably; third, the relationship can go to the next collaring level. A Collar of Consideration is a serious step, and it sends a signal to other Doms that the couple has begun a relationship. In vanilla-speak this is a *serious dating* stage where you're each trying to determine how well you might fit together without over-committing yourselves.

Training Collar—Most common use: The *training collar* often comes next, and is roughly analogous to an engagement ring. Before moving to this level of collar, most couples have spent a substantial amount of time discussing mutual likes, dislikes, needs and wishes. At this level, both parties are considering the real possibility that this relationship may grow into a permanent union, and the D-type is now *training* the s-type in the specific behaviors that will be expected should the relationship continue. This is the shake-down cruise—the *dress rehearsal.*

There are some fine points that now relate to each party:
- Before accepting the collar, the s-type should already understand what is expected from a relationship with this D-type.
- Once collared at this level, the s-type's behavior (in public, on the phone, on Internet sites) reflects directly upon the Dominant.
- The D-type is now responsible for this person. Unless pre-negotiated, the D-type would no longer have close relationships with other submissives.
- The s-type may struggle with submission and

commitment to one person. The s-type is no longer available to other D-types, and in this and other ways, may feel that his/her personal freedoms are being restricted (which, in fact, they are).

This collar indicates a deepening relationship in which the Dom is teaching the submissive about the ways he or she wishes to be served. At this level, either party may end the relationship, but the break is much more public, serious, and painful for both parties.

Training Collar—alternate use: A D-type serving as a *mentor* may place a training collar on an s-type who is being trained in correct behavior and protocols until a suitable D-type partner can be found for the mentee. That collar remains with the s-type until that suitable D-type is found. The mentor usually helps in the search, guiding and steering the s-type during the quest. While collared, this submissive is treated as if owned by the mentoring Dominant. As with protection collars, it is usually a Dominant of high standing and respect that becomes a mentor.

Permanent Collar (or slave Collar): The final collar is usually referred to as a *permanent collar* or a *slave collar.* This is considered by many to be analogous to a wedding band, and the submissive/slave is now regarded as the formally owned by their Dominant/Master. At this stage, the collar is considered permanent and would only be removed by the D-type for some exceptional reason. The slave would not have the authority to remove the collar, and doing so (unless required by some dire necessity) would end the relationship. At this stage, the D-type cannot release a slave for any aspect of service failure, for that would indicate the D-type's failure to train more than the slave's failure to serve.

Special-use collars

Scene collar: Some Tops place a scene collar around the bottom's neck as a symbol of the Top's dominance during the scene. This is only appropriate when the bottom is an uncollared submissive. For years, I used a lovely piece of black lace ribbon as a scene collar: I have it to this day.

Collar of Protection (may be called a House Collar): When new to the community, it can be intimidating for a young woman to go alone to a BDSM play party where their newness can draw uncomfortable attention. There is a process within our community for helping ease newcomers into social settings: they may seek (or be offered) protection from an established Dominant—usually someone well known and of high standing. There is no time limit on a collar of protection; it is there for as long as it is needed.

When wearing a Collar of Protection, Dom/mes who wish to communicate with this person—whether by e-mail, FetLife, or in person—must first obtain permission from the protecting Dominant.

Sometimes, a submissive asks for a Collar of Protection after a failed or abusive relationship, or because she's having some difficulty with one or more people in the community. The Collar of Protection provides time for the submissive to heal emotionally and to attend local BDSM events without having Doms approach her without permission.

The Velcro collar

This term is usually applied to online relationships where one or the other partner has a series of fairly brief collared relationships. In real-time relationships, the term *Velcro collar* refers to a Dom/Master (or sub/slave) who extends (or accepts) a collar without much thought about the commitment and obligations that accompany a symbol of such significance. Bad experiences with clueless Doms/Maters (or subs/slaves) drives many people from this way of life with broken hearts and a very distorted experience of what BDSM is all about.

The Invisible Collar

My partner and co-author created the term *invisible collar* to describe the lingering emotional connection between people after an emotionally bonding experience that does not end decisively. It doesn't matter whether the emotionally bonding experience is a single intense scene or a months- or years-long intense personal relationship. What seems to matter is that there was not a clearly understood end.

She coined the phrase after recognizing some common patterns emerging from discussions about M/s relationship break-ups. In particular, Jen noticed that people who had been involved in intense relationships that had ended with *closure* reported very different post-relationship experiences than did people whose relationships had just fizzled away.

While *huge* emotional pain and trauma often come with the end of relationships, it seemed that people got over their break-ups much faster when those relationships had been ended with dignity and formality. In fact, many people admitted that when they had been in relationships that had ended without closure, they often felt a lingering connection that could last for many months or even years. During that agonizing time of unresolved separation, one or both of the previous partners would want to call/contact/reach out to the other person. Many people said they continued to think about the way the relationship had ended and wished that they could have done something differently to have prevented the break-up. These people reported that the other person was often on their mind and that this period was a slow emotional torture.

Jen coined the term *invisible collar* to describe the long-lasting tug (or pull) towards a prior relationship partner long after they had expected those feelings to go away. She and I discussed the concept quite a bit and realized that the *invisible collar* concept ties in with the way one ends a scene with people other than regular committed partners.
- You enter an interaction (either for a meeting, a scene, or even a brief relationship) with purpose and intent.
- When the meeting/scene/relationship is over, you either have or have not fulfilled your purpose and intent.
- To the extent that something is left unfinished, to the extent that you feel that the connection did not resolve completely, you may be left with a *psychological connection* that may take longer to fade than you expected.

That's the Invisible Collar.

A quick word about protocols

Protocols and Rituals

In the military sense, *protocols* are a directed series of steps to follow in a given situation to create a defined, reproducible result. There are protocols for making your bunk, saluting senior officers, and for defusing a bomb. In business, there are protocols for conducting a financial audit and for drawing up a corporate balance sheet. This list is endless.

In the world of BDSM there are two general categories of protocols: personal protocols and scene protocols.

Personal protocols (that are outgrowths of the D-type's values) are often used within an authority-based relationship (such as a Master/slave relationship) as a way to create an effective *governance structure*. Protocols are less common in D/s structures because the D-type's authority over the s-type is more limited.

In a general sense, slave's personal protocols reflect how Master wishes slave to behave in various settings and how Master wants certain things done. Master will establish differing sets of protocols for different slaves in their service: protocols are relationship-specific. If you wish to read more about personal protocols, I've listed some books in Supplement B: Core Readings for Master/slave. Bear in mind, I've written an entire book devoted to personal protocols in Master/slave relationships.

Scene protocols refer to the rules of courtesy that apply when a bunch of kinksters get together at a play party or in a public dungeon. I discussed these in detail in the first book in this BDSM Mastery series.

Rituals set the tone for something that is about to happen or is happening. You get to ritual through theatrics that involve as many senses as possible. *Rituals* are often used in authority-imbalanced relationships to set the stage for repeated events that involve focus and bonding. There can be rituals before scenes, there can be rituals when one partner comes home from work.

Rituals help build expectations and focus your anticipation on the impending event; they bring ceremony to the event and fill it with memories. Most commonly, rituals are a series of activities (often governed by protocols) strung together into a sequence that represents a preferred way doing something. For example, you may have a *dining elegantly at home* ritual that includes having cocktails before dinner in your living room while there is a fire burning in the fireplace. Within that ritual, you may many *protocols* that concern who sets the fireplace, how the fireplace is set, who lights the fireplace, and when it gets lit. You may have many protocols about how the appetizers and cocktails are prepared and served and how the lights, candles and music are set up.

Rituals are powerful things. The ways you celebrate Christmas Eve or Christmas Day, New Years Eve, or Thanksgiving are all examples of rituals. You would be shocked if a ritual didn't match the tradition you'd learned to associate with it. Think about your reaction if you walked into your mother's home for Easter Dinner to find a Christmas tree set up and decorated with presents scattered below? Wrong ritual; the *Christmas Tree Ritual* isn't due for another eight or nine months. You'd be so disturbed by this that you'd immediately call every member of your family about seeking psychiatric help for her.

Protocols and rituals play important roles in our world. In public (perhaps at a munch or at a play party) they help us to identify others who play in our particular little puddle. (Do you wear a bar vest to a munch or play party? Are you all dressed in black? Are you wearing blue jeans or black jeans? Etc.) In a relationship, they are used to increase interpersonal bonding every bit as much as they shape the look and feel of the ways partners interacts. (Who is walking in the lead? Who is opening doors for whom? Who is saying, "Yes, Sir" or "Yes, Master?" Protocols.

Chapter 6
Now—bringing this all together

So, where are we? With any luck at all, I've given you some new ideas to consider. In this chapter, I'm going to revisit and expand upon a few of those ideas and then add a few others—just to keep you interested in this material and this Very Unusual Culture (as A.A. Milne would punctuate it if this were a story about Christopher Robin and Winnie the Pooh).

This is the chapter that some of you may need to set aside until you've been doing this a while. This is the chapter that you can give to a more experienced friend to read and evaluate so you can find out whether this is really so, or whether I'm really off somewhere in lala land.

While the first two sections of this chapter do, in fact, build off the material you've been reading, the third and fourth sections do not: they add new ideas.

Additional Hints about Kinky Relationships (the third section) sounds some relationship and communication warning bells. If you would like to read much more about communication issues in authority-imbalanced relationships, I'd suggest two of my other books:
- *Master/slave Relations: Communications 401—The Advanced Course.* Las Vegas: Nazca Plains, 2007.
- *Master/slave Relations: Solutions 402—Living in Harmony.* Las Vegas: Nazca Plains, 2007.

Introducing Some New (Interesting) Concepts (the fourth and final section) is much more advanced than material that you're likely to run into in most other BDSM books. By way of tantalizing you, my purpose in writing this last section is to expose you to some complex ideas so you can think about them over time. Said differently, I'm not going to take time in this book to fully develop some of the statements/ideas in this section, I'm just making them available to you. Also, some of these statements are really *assertions*. These are views or opinions that I have developed over time that I believe are worth sharing with you but remain, at their core, simply my own views or opinions.

So, here we go.

Revisiting and expanding some of the key concepts from this book

You're getting to the end of this book and I'd like to draw some conclusions from what you've been reading. This is the part of the book where I can give you some material to think about.

Authority-based relationships
Authority-based relationships (even more than power exchange relationships) differ from vanilla relationships in many ways, of course, but for me, one characteristic stands out above the rest: the degree of communication. The extensive negotiations/discussions that result in this type of relationship, combined with the requirement for extensive, clear ongoing discussions to keep the relationship going, seem to unite couples in ways that are particularly strong from a mental health perspective. The D/s, M/s, O/p, or TPE (Total Power Exchange) couple's very awareness of (and agreement upon) their roles and responsibilities—topics generally *assumed* or *left invisible* in most relationships—seems to put them in a class unto themselves.

Eyes wide shut?
Some people consider BDSM-based relationships to be a cover for maintaining an abusive (*nonconsensual*) relationship. These people believe that BDSM-based relationships are inherently unhealthy and disadvantageous for the s-type. This misses the point that consent is

the cornerstone of BDSM; the s-type enters into a role knowing who holds the power and who makes what decisions. As it relates to many authority-based roles in life (any role where you have a boss), *liking it* has nothing to do with it; obedience has everything to do with it.

Sometimes, one or both partners specifically seek some of the items on the *checklist of abusive behaviors* for reasons unique to their own backgrounds. This is one of the reasons the vanilla community can have such a difficult time understanding BDSM-based relationships. In the same way that people say that beauty is in the eye of the beholder, they also say that one man's trash is another man's treasure. Oh, and for those of you who play the stock market, please consider this: the stock you think is at such a great place to buy must—by definition—be considered by the seller to be at a great place to sell (or you wouldn't be able to make the buy, right?). I ran a commodity futures brokerage company for a number of years and found that clients had a hard time grasping the implications of a very simple concept: one of you must be dead wrong.

Trust in relationships: acts of omission and commission

An act of commission is doing something that you know you should not do; an act of omission is NOT doing something that you know you should do. Most people in a relationship view omission and commission as equal trust violations, as they represent failures to protect your partner's feelings.

Failing to protect your partner's trust can be deadly in a relationship. My partner, Jen, puts it this way: "Imagine *trust* as a fresh sheet of paper. Think of *broken trust* as that piece of paper being crumpled. Even if you iron the crumpled paper in an effort to make it look fresh and new, it will never again look like it was before it was crumpled. Your word is your bond and it is all you have in this world; be careful how you pledge your word." To which I add: daily you have a chance to practice living up to your word: drive the speed limit—it's part of your Social Compact. Be places when you say you'll be there—you've given your word. The more you are able to keep your word on small issues, the more easily you'll find it to keep your word on large issues. You'll have developed the habit of being reliable.

As they each represent dishonesty, continued acts of commission or omission can be grounds for ending a relationship. If serious enough, one single act may break apart a couple even after many years together. As an example, I am friends with a senior Leatherman who precipitously ended a 15-year relationship with his partner for violating the *no-illegal-substances-ever* pledge in their contract. My friend discovered his slave stoned on drugs. Gut-wrenching as it was, the D-type ordered his s-type partner to remove all his property and leave within 24 hours. Think about it: what was the option? How could the s-type place future trust the D-type's integrity if that D-type had relented and agreed to overlook the s-type's moral lapse?

Some special notes about relationships

Stripped to basic concepts, relationships can be seen to have three components: *structure, sex practices,* and *beliefs.* For those of us who live in the world of BDSM and Leather, our structure is described as M/s or D/s (or husband/wife or Daddy/boy, etc) and also includes the depth and breadth of *service* associated with such roles, SM refers to our sex practices, and terms such as *vanilla, BDSM,* and *Leather* describes our values and beliefs. (No, this isn't the book to explain *Leather,* sorry. I've listed some books in Supplement B.)

Some relationship notes for D-types
The person who gives him/herself to you is a volunteer. They—like you—have stepped out of the Land of Vanillas and are exploring. They may be exploring with you or they may be exploring on their own and only briefly touch your life. They are a gift, yet—as PhoenixRed points out—you are a gift for them. They have found something in you that sings to their hearts, but you are providing the song. You may not understand their reasons for choosing you, for *they* may not be aware of their reasons.

In fact, one of the great risks for those who are young and not yet emotionally mature (or sexually experienced) is that they don't know what they're looking for or what to expect from a relationship even if they find one. Their dreams and fantasies get mixed up with the excitement of new and intense stimulation. For some, this leads to clarifying personal insights; for others, it leads to emotional confusion.

Once you have been involved with BDSM for a number of years and have invested a lot of time and effort into learning SM and D/s skills, please choose an s-type worthy of the investment you've made in yourself. Specifically, after you have spent time with your potential partner, after you've gone through your relationship negotiations, it's your responsibility as the Dom/me to decide whether or not you will accept someone as your sub even if the sub really wants to be with you. The Dom/me has the right to refuse their gift if they feel that this simply isn't the right gift. Each of us has the final say on whom we choose as a partner for the particular relationship structure we envision.

Some relationship notes for s-types

The gift you offer a Dom/me or Master is priceless, but you must be careful with whom you share the gift of yourself. There are many good people in our community who have not yet learned to be wise and responsible Dominants within our culture. These people have not yet learned to responsibly control the power that they are given by your submission. While they can love you very much, they can hurt you far more than they understand. I urge you to reserve your service for someone who has at least learned the basics of power-exchange relationships *and is clearly trying to learn more*. If your intended Dom/me is **not** clearly trying to learn more, they should seek a mentor before you ever submit to him… or her.

Power exchange versus authority transfer

There are two common situations where these terms are used: *play scenes* that involve power dynamics (as opposed to play scenes that are intended as skills practice) and *relationships*.

Play scenes: When a couple (or more, but that's more advanced) decides to *do* a scene, someone is directing that scene—obviously. If it's a skill-training scene that has no psychological component, that person is referred to as the Top. However, if the scene is going to involve a psychological dynamic, then the Top is also described as the Dominant. There are *power exchange* techniques that the Dom/

me can use when starting a scene that give it more depth. Succinctly, power exchange comes into play when people negotiate a scene and the submissive agrees to give the Dominant the power to control the scene and also what is done to their body—within the negotiated boundaries.

The term *authority transfer* is used to describe how *personal power* is handled in certain types of relationships:

- In M/s and O/p structures, the slave (in exchange for total protection and care) has *transferred personal authority over itself to its Master/Owner*, who then has absolute *authority* over every aspect of the s-type's life. For all practical purposes, there are only moral/ethical/legal limits to the D-type's authority when the relationship is based on this degree of authority transfer.
- In D/s structures, the Dominant may have complete authority over specifically negotiated areas of a submissive's life, but that Dominant will only have *influence* over areas not directly under the Dom's authority.

Additional hints about kinky relationships

You can only get back as much as you put out

Your own energy level strongly influences the energy level of those with whom you are interacting. Humans have a strong tendency to mirror those around them. By extension, the energy that you put out when you go to a munch, club meeting, or play party directly influences the energy others reflect back to you. If you're introverted and those looking at you see by your posture that you're not open, you may not meet any/many people, and when you look around others are likely to reflect your own mood/behavior back to you. Others will be socializing, but people may not be quick to include you because you're radiating barbs and prickles. You're likely to come away from a meeting feeling that the club members are standoffish and cliquish.

On the other hand, if you open yourself up and are smiling and gregarious you'll likely meet smiling and gregarious people. As a general rule of life, happy people looking for happy people meet happy people; people who are unhappy about themselves to the point that it shows don't meet many people.

Tip: You might keep this saying in mind: "It's better to be interested than interesting." You'll make a lot more friends that way.

Tip: Learn to calm your eye movement. Keep your eyes from jumping around when you're speaking with someone. Focus on a point on their face and lock your eyes there. This is particularly important if the person you're speaking with is naked.

Tip: To help remember someone's name, imagine writing it on their forehead with a red marking pen as soon as you hear them say it. Then use it immediately when addressing them. If you can use it three times, chances are you'll remember it.

Tip: Do some reading and research BEFORE going to a group's event so that you have the confidence to ask intelligent questions and fit comfortably into conversations. By the way, if you're to this point in this book and have not yet gone to a munch, chances are that you'll have as much or more knowledge (not experience, but knowledge) about BDSM as most of the other people in the room.

New-relationship train wrecks

For those new to the BDSM culture, I hear about one particular relationship scenario more often than any other. It's the case where the relationship starts out with intense sex and fabulous power-exchange scenes—often Master/slave scenes. Master is ordering the slave to do things and the slave is having a marvelous time being a slave and serving the Master. A nice continuation from the Internet play they're used to. After about three months, the New Relationship Energy (NRE) starts to wear off and *things start to change*. Master is no longer assigning tasks for slave; Master isn't noticing that slave is not doing everything that it was asked to do. The slave misses being punished for failing to correctly complete tasks.

The slave feels as though Master has gone away. The relationship continues to be warm and loving, the sex continues to be frequent and hot, but the fulfillment that had been provided by the Master/slave side of the equation seems to have drifted away. Neither Master nor slave feel that this is the deal they had signed up for.

There can be any number of reasons why the focus shifts in a relationship. For example:

- The couple may have been living in fantasy. They hadn't read/studied about how to set up a 24/7 Master/slave structure and hadn't realized how serious and challenging it can be: it's a lot of work and Master is getting worn out directing the slave—or slave has concluded it's not a slave, at least not for this Master.
- The D-type has fallen in love with the s-type and now has feelings for the s-type that conflict with the D-type's own values about how to treat a woman. As the D-type pulls the relationship back to the safety of a boyfriend/girlfriend vanilla model, the s-type becomes alarmed and asks: "Where did my Master go?"

This line of thought brings up another point that PhoenixRed has mentioned. Couples new to Master/slave may start out *scening* the roles without actually speaking about making it a way of life for themselves. They *assumed* that the role-play would naturally transfer into a daily living dynamic without discussing how to do that. They skipped the *taking it to the next level* negotiation.

In these situations, it might help if the couple sat down and each wrote a detailed description of what the **roles** of *being a Dom/Owner* and *being a slave, submissive* means to them. Next, do the same exercise but describe what degree of control the D-type envisions having over the s-type and the degree of control the s-type sees the D-type exercising over him/her. The goal is to open discussions about the degree of control the s-type wishes the D-type to assume over him/her—and also the degree of control the D-type wishes to exert over the s-type. Translation: one person may want to be more controlled than the other person wishes to provide.

It takes hard work and open communication to keep these kinds of intense relationships going. Also, the kind of compassionate leadership that is called for is not normally taught to people; they either have lived long enough to figure it out or they have to be committed to reading/ learning about interpersonal communication and team leadership. Relationships always take work, but authority-based relationships take a *lot* of work.

Thoughtful and ethical personnel leadership and management are serious topics that require training and experience. That's one reason there are more followers than leaders in businesses—and why the leaders are paid more.

Overfeeding a fetish can kill it

Some people develop almost instant bonds once the two of them find a fetish in common. One is a sadist, one is a masochist: a match. One is a *little* the other is a *Daddy*: a match. They both like *Leather*: a match. One likes to lead and be a dominant, one likes to follow a leader and have the leader take care of them: *a D/s match.*

At least they're a match for a while. To the extent that you're together primarily because of your shared fetish, there is risk. To the extent that each of you have outside interests and broad interests outside your fetish (or kink preferences) you'll be a strong couple.

Message: if you find a partner from within the BDSM world, don't forget some of the lessons you learned in your prior vanilla life: relationships thrive on fresh and diverse ideas and activities.

Let's say that one of you likes to be flogged and the other likes to flog; you're a good match and everything is working out well. But you've moved from playing at play parties to moving in together and now you're doing flogging play scenes many times a week. Because the bottom is getting used to the way you flog and the feel of your floggers, the bottom is asking for more. The bottom wants to be struck harder or with more vicious floggers. At some point, you come face-to-face with the reality that if you go much further, you'll be stripping skin off the bottom's back. So you guys lose interest in flogging and floggers.

Message: Too much of a good thing is still too much. (I picked on floggers as something that is easy to understand: to make it more real in your mind, think about rough body play. After a while, you'll be worried about breaking bones.)

Transference and Projection

In psychology, *transference* refers to the unconscious process of redirecting feelings about one person to another person. For instance, you might mistrust somebody who shares some of your ex-spouse's manners, voice, or external appearance. Conversely, you may be overly compliant to someone who resembles one of your parents or someone you have long respected as an authority figure.

Psychological *projection* (or projection bias) is the term used to describe an ego defense mechanism wherein you attribute (or *project*) your own unacceptable or unwanted thoughts or/and emotions to another person. This occurs because you're sensitive to (dislike) some aspect of your own behavior and when you see someone else exhibiting somewhat similar behavior, you may react negatively to that person even though this other person hasn't yet done anything to demonstrate unworthiness or distrust.)

For example, projection occurs when Person A projects his/her own interpretation of an act onto Person B and then reacts to Person B *as if* they had reacted as Person A imagined that they did. This situation can occur when one person is not listening carefully to another, when one person is guilty about something and is trying to shift the blame, or when a person projects personal insecurities or weaknesses onto the other partner and then reacts to those projections.

Worse, the person being blamed is not at fault. Either there has been some serious breach of trust perceived by the person doing the blaming or the person doing the blaming is personally insecure about something and is lashing out.

- If the projection concerns a perceived breach of trust of your partner, you probably have a communications challenge.
- If the projection is not specific and occurs rather randomly, it may well result from low self-esteem. In that case, the one doing the projecting is likely to have a lot of personal work to do.

It doesn't take a rocket scientist to realize that once one person starts reacting to their own projected insecurities, the relationship has headed down a path filled with misunderstandings, hurt feelings, and mutual bitterness.

If one partner's projections go unchecked, both partners will increasingly grow wary of one another. One partner is seeing dragons under the bed while the other partner can't figure out what they did to trigger this negative pattern.

Introducing some new (interesting) concepts

We're now at the point in this book that I can share some of the more interesting ideas and topics that relate to experiences you're likely to have once you've been at it for a few years.

Not all of this material will resonate with you right now. Over the years that you walk this path, more and more of the material in this particular chapter will make sense to you. Remember: some of the material in here expresses my own opinions or viewpoints. I apologize in advance if it hits you the wrong way. Remember: I'm a lot older than you. A lot older.

Why High Protocol Master/slave Relationships work

Master/slave relationships are often seen as one of the edgier relationship structures that a couple can choose. In an M/s structure, you have one person transferring authority over himself or herself to another person to whom they have sworn total obedience and service. Think of a king and a vassal.

Sometimes, when I'm discussing or describing Master/slave structures to those unfamiliar with them, they express opinions ranging from offended shock to skepticism. Who in this day and age, they will ask, would willingly turn authority of themselves over to another? Why, in this day and age of enlightened free choice, would a person living in this land of unlimited opportunities surrender personal control in order to dedicate himself or herself to the service of Another?

Good questions.

I've thought about this a great deal; I've lived in Master/slave structures for over ten years. There are many answers, of course, for people have unknowable motivations to do things. Some of us are simply more comfortable being led by someone we believe to be an inspired and loving leader. Some of us don't have the sense to come in out of the rain and have found someone who will bring us inside. Some of us...

But, those are the stories we tell ourselves; those are the superficial reasons we use to explain why we would live this way. Recently, I was able to work out the larger connection between authority-based relationships and Western Civilization in a way that helps me to understand not only why Master/slave relationships work, but also why many of us feel that they are so natural.

So, here's what I think...

Historians reading this section will get this immediately; if you're not a British history buff, you'll either have to take my word for it or do some research. The fact is, British culture—as it evolved from Anglo Saxon roots in the Dark Ages—was based on four core concepts: *discipline, hierarchy, efficiency,* and *law.*

While civilizations throughout the world honor these concepts to some degree or another, the stunning thing is... these four concepts are represent the basis for the *Leather* version of a high-protocol, authority-based relationship. To make this connection clear, I've simply added the word or phrase that would be used among M/s couples that translates these centuries-old concepts into modern English:
- Discipline (obedience)
- Hierarchy (authority-based relationships)
- Efficiency (protocols)
- Law (accountability: consequences for actions)

I assert that this form of relationship—the M/s form of relationship—resonates with many people because it touches upon the very foundations of our cultural heritage in a way that vanilla marriages do not. While vanilla marriages may contain some/most/all of these components, they do so only accidentally: they are not up-front direct conditions of a traditional marriage in Western Civilization in the 21st Century. But these conditions *are* the up-front direct conditions of most/all Master/slave relationships.

This is not the book to expand this idea. If you are interested in learning more about the Master/slave subculture, I've included some references in the Supplement.

Presence and mindfulness

Our reality is made up of consecutive moments of *now*. After all, there is nothing else but *now* and then another *now* and then another. Together, they make up the movie of your life. This movie is influenced by all the experiences and baggage that you've been accumulating since birth. Literally, you've been accumulating this baggage since your first day of life.

Now is the only opportunity you have to interact with others. After all, you can't interact with someone five minutes ago, you can't get back to the exact conditions that existed between you and anything else five minutes ago. So, you can't take back what you said five minutes ago. If you stuck your foot in your mouth, your only option is to chew it—now.

So what?

The *so what* is that I'm making a plea to you to come present and be mindful in your life. Great books have been written simply on these concepts; one of my favorite books related to *mindfulness* is titled: *How to Train a Wild Elephant and Other Lessons in Mindfulness* (Jan Chozen Bays, 2011). In the context of this book, the path toward being present and mindful relates directly to the quality of your SM play experiences as well as the quality of your personal relationships. After all, your thoughts and actions are most purposeful when you are fully *in the present* and paying attention to your own thoughts and actions. Because themes such as these are woven in to book, presentations, and demos on BDSM, it has been my experience that BDSM-based relationships seem to be both more intense and more varied than most vanilla relationships that I've heard about. I urge you to learn something about techniques to help you be present in this world—and mindful of your actions.

As a side note, I'll add the comment that one comes to appreciate the reason behind one's behaviors, emotions, and reactions by learning to be mindful and introspective. However, it is much harder than you might think actually to sustain a mindful state of being and to integrate it into your personality. That said, your ability to be present and mindful will have a gigantic influence on your connection with your partner whether you are having an SM scene or having dinner.

Needs versus wants

Part of the trick of assessing a possible relationship is to separate your *needs* from your *wants* and then to try to determine what it will cost you in time, effort, and money to get from where you are to where you want to be. One time, when I worked for the research division of the U.S. Department of Justice, a senior executive made a comment that will remain with me all my life. I consider it to be one of life's more amusing truths.

> What you have is not what you want,
> What you want is not what you need, and
> What you need costs too much.

So: if it appears that you are not happy in your life or in a relationship, you might wish to reassess your needs. You may have everything that you want but not everything that you need. And trust me; the costs of getting what you need can be very high. I'm speaking from experience.

Holding space: To *hold space* means that when someone you care about is going through a difficult period, you provide/maintain a stable, solid ground for them to work through their issue(s) without adding any judgment, criticism or blame. To hold space is to create a neutral territory for the other to just... be. This is your assurance to the other person that you have faith in their intelligence to figure out the right solution/path on their own. This is the opposite of giving advice, taking a pill to mask a symptom, or rushing to get to an outcome.

From PhoenixRed's perspective as a senior Domme, holding space may also mean putting the SM activities on the back burner or taking a break from the BDSM relationship altogether in order to focus on important life issues.

Intent versus *content* in communication

Interpersonal communication takes place concurrently at two levels: content and intent. The *content* is what you're speaking about while the *intent* is the context, or container, within which you are speaking. The success or failure to communicate content is heavily influenced by your conscious/subconscious intent.

Intent can itself be divided into two styles: *controlling/supportive* and *defensive/learning*. I don't want to get sidetracked into an academic discussion about communication intricacies, but I *do* want to alert you to the key variables by posing some questions:

- Are you saying what you are saying to support the other person, to deliver neutral facts, or to control the other person in some way?
- Are you listening to understand or are you listening to defend your position?

How you construct and control what you say, how you phrase it, your tone of voice and your word choice matters as much or more than the content. All of these variables combine to strongly impact the quality of your personal life and the success/failure of your relationship(s).

Distinctions such as these are important if you're intending to have a *peak experience* with someone. For starters, you might want to spend a few minutes teasing apart what you even mean by a *peak experience*, then go on to figure out what a *peak experience* is for YOU. How do you identify the elements of *having the best time, ever*? You might start by describing how your *best time* affects your five senses. Now, beyond the five senses, how do you identify what really pleases you? Perhaps an Internet search on topics such as: *test what makes you happy* is in your future.

Male/Female morality

While not often discussed, the way men and women are socialized in the U.S. seems also to be reflected in the different ways that men and women judge moral issues. While not substantiated by research of any kind, my own experiences support the observation that men tend to weigh actions on a scale of good or bad *consequences* while women tend to weigh actions on a scale of good or bad *intentions*. Male morality tends to value honor, integrity, loyalty, and trust, while female morality seems to emphasize trust, kindness, humility, and sympathy. These differences can be important in an authority-imbalanced relationship for it suggests that at a very basic level, the male and female partners are seeking/judging different signals from the other person as they each are building the foundation of trust upon which the entire relationship rests.

First, if there is a male D-type and female s-type, there may be differences in the ways they value some actions—and those differences can lead to friction or relationship stress. Second, if the structure is one of a female D-type with a male s-type, Master may be steering the relationship in ways that are unfamiliar and possibly difficult for the s-type to understand.

Message: unlike the majority of authority-equal relationship structures (boyfriend/girlfriend; husband/wife), authority-imbalanced relationship structures are inherently more thought provoking and cerebral—and involve much more communication.

PhoenixRed has shared an interesting perspective about the *intent* of vanilla versus BDSM relationships. She says that in her experience and observations, vanilla males enter into relationships thinking in terms of what they are giving up (time with their friends, money, etc.), whereas vanilla women enter into relationships looking at what they are going to gain (security, intimacy, etc.). However, she also observes, it's different in BDSM relationships. In BDSM relationships, the D- and s-types both have to consider what they are going to gain and what they are going to have to give up. This is especially true in FemDomme/male-submissive dynamics, because in that dynamic both people are bucking the gender norms of what society says is right and moral.

Wishing you the very best

You've come to the end of the book.

Before I leave you, let me say again: a decision to participate in the BDSM way of life is a decision to be transformed in some way. Some will be careful and fortunate and will be rewarded by finding what Guy Baldwin refers to as *ecstatic erotic catharsis*. Some will find themselves caught up in intense relationships, yet over time discover that their reasons for participating in this edgy form of sexuality are not good reasons. Some will *not* take to heart the guidance, cautions, and admonitions that you've been reading in this book and will—unfortunately—discover that their participation in the BDSM community has actually made them more wary and less trusting of others and may cause them to leave the BDSM world more isolated and miserable than they were initially.

Please be aware: while most who enter find a welcome home, others who enter are not as fortunate. As with most complex projects, the more time and effort you put into studying and exploring, the more you'll get out of it.

Which brings us to a central Truth about being a human: In your life, progress is a choice. You can stay intellectually, emotionally, socially, physically, and fiscally as you are, or you can choose to continue to learn and grow. Personal growth is just that—personal. The aphorism that expresses this thought so succinctly is: *If it's going to be, it's up to me.*

I've presented a terrific amount of material for you in this book and I suspect that it will take you some time to digest all of it. I've included an Supplement to help you to your next level of research. I have no doubt that quite soon you will find someone and want to play with them; quite soon you'll find someone and you'll want to go beyond play to form a relationship. It is for the *you* who are at that stage on your BDSM Path that this book has been written.

May the wind be always at your back.

In Leather Heart and Spirit,

Bob

Supplements

Supplement A: Glossary of Selected Terms

Authority-based relationships: Relationships where one person is clearly the leader and the other is clearly subordinate. Among the more common structures listed here, this book mostly describes D/s relationships.

- Dominant/submissive (D/s)
- Master/slave (M/s)
- Owner/property (O/p)
- TPE (Total Power Exchange).

BDSM represents a continuum of practices and expressions, both erotic and non-erotic, involving restraint, sensory stimulation, role-playing, and a variety of interpersonal dynamics. The term *BDSM* is an abbreviation of: **B**ondage/**D**iscipline; **D**ominance/**s**ubmission; **S**ado**M**asochism.

Dominant and *submissive* (**Dom** and **sub** or **D-type** and **s-type**) are terms that relate to behaviors linked to personality traits; you could as easily substitute the terms *leader* and *follower*.

Dom and Domme: the shorthand male and female version of the word *dominant*. Generally, when I write *Dom* the person can be of either gender. When the topic specifically concerns a female dominant I will use *Domme*. A female dominant is not to be confused with a domineering female. A domineering female (sometimes called a *bitch*) **expects** service while a dominant of either gender **accepts** service in the context of their role as the dominant leader.

D/s play or D/s scenes: play/scenes (terms I use interchangeably) with or without SM toys/tools that involves the power exchange component of dominance and submission: includes physical play, psychological play, and role play.

D/s scenes with sadistic/masochistic preferences–Combining: A *dominant* (Dom or D-type) and a *submissive* (sub or s-type) may have either sadistic or masochistic erotic preferences. Most commonly, those with dominant personalities *give* strong sensations to others, but every so often you will find a strong D-type who has connected sexual pleasure from *receiving* those strong (possibly painful) sensations.

Gor: short for *Gorean*—a subculture that grew out of the science fiction novels of John Norman based on a belief that in the natural order of things, males are inherently dominant over females. Although rare, there are communities who live according to Gorean customs much as there are communities who live according to some aspect of BDSM customs.

Kinky: slang for people who enjoy *adventuresome sex*, which is, itself, a euphemism for BDSM.

Kinsey scale: The 0-6 Kinsey scale (also called the Heterosexual-Homosexual Rating Scale) attempts to describe a person's sexual preferences. In this scale, zero means that the person is exclusively heterosexual and six means that the person is exclusively homosexual. Someone who is bisexual would be a 3 or 4.

Leather, Leathermen, Leathersex: The Leather subculture is one of many facets of semi-organized alternative sexuality. In recent decades the Leather community has almost come to be viewed as a subset of BDSM culture rather than a descendant of gay culture. Almost anything that is said about Leather and its evolution to present times is subject to challenge, so to avoid controversy I've simply listed some resources in the Supplement so you'll have places to look for more information if you are interested.

Master and slave: usually applied to a 24/7 relationship structure wherein the subordinate person (slave) has surrendered authority over themselves and pledged to serve and to obey their Master who now exerts total control and offers total protection for this person.

Munch: Munches are intended to be non-threatening social gatherings to help those who are curious about BDSM meet others who may be able to help them become more comfortable and better informed. Munches can also be a place to get advice about BDSM experiences.

Negotiating/negotiations: The process of determining what will and will not go on in a play scene—or in a relationship. As some people consider the scene to start with negotiations, this is not a time to be interrupted.

Old Guard: A term used to describe a near-mythical time in gay Leather history when returned GIs from World War II blended some features of their military experiences with their kinky interests to produce a subculture that over time became known as *Leather*. Some of the distant echoes of their quasi-military rules of protocol, inclusion, and exclusion can still be seen in today's BDSM society.

Sadism: in psychiatry, the condition in which sexual gratification depends on causing pain or degradation to others.

SM: sadomasochism (I use caps for these letters in this book). The psychological tendency or sexual practice characterized by both sadism and masochism.

SM play/scenes: activities between two or more people of any gender that involve giving and receiving sensations such as spanking, flogging, whipping, etc. for their mutual and consensual enjoyment.

SM techniques: methods such as spanking, whipping, bondage, or electro-stimulation that sadists may use to cause masochists to feel the desired sensations.

SSC: Safe, Sane, and Consensual—A slogan used to summarize the minimal physical/psychological conditions most people consider acceptable for SM play to take place.

Safe-call: a procedure used when meeting someone for the first time (or even when meeting someone that you don't know well) that ensures that someone else knows what you're doing, where you'll be doing it, and that you are safely.

Sex-role stereotyping: The general public stereotype is that Doms are men with sadistic/Top preferences and that submissives are women who have masochistic/bottom preferences. These are stereotypes and are far from the way roles are practiced within this culture. In reality, Dominants can be male or female, masochists or sadists and of any sexual orientation. So can submissives.

Submissive versus slave

Note: Once again, I caution readers that the characteristics listed under *submissive* and *slave* are generalizations based on my own research and experiences living within (and studying) the field of BDSM and Master/slave relations since 2001. These descriptions are certainly not intended to be taken as *rules*. These are my own distinctions and may not be generally accepted by others practicing D/s or M/s structures. As you, yourself, grow in BDSM experience, what I write in this book generally—and the following points about distinctions between *submissive* and *slave* specifically—may make more sense to you.

I'll begin by proposing that *submissive* and *slave* motivations and behaviors aren't quite the same. While one is certainly not better than the other, one set of behaviors is more likely to fit some people than others.

submissive

- D/s relationship is based on power *exchange* (meaning that the submissive who normally has personal authority over their what they, themselves, may or may not do or have done to them can give or exchange that power to the Dom/me for a prescribed period)
- submissives have a strong desire to serve—but under certain negotiated conditions.
- Typically, the negotiated area include the submissive's terms of service, the length of that service, the hard and soft limits, and the safewords.
- The submissive will also negotiate those aspects of their life that the Dom doesn't control. These aspects often include the submissive's biological family and children, work, education and religious observance.
- The conditions under which the submissive is willing to serve can be renegotiated (This is a major issue: the submissive retains the personal authority to ask their Dominant to

renegotiate their terms of service, but the Dominant is under no obligation to accept the newly proposed conditions.)

- If the Dom breaks the submissives hard limits, the scene would end and—in the case of a breach of a relationship trust—the relationship could end.

- The Dom may be permitted to break *soft limits* (things the submissive has said they really aren't interested in) after discussing it with the submissive and obtaining their permission.

- In many/most cases, submissives cross back and forth between retaining and surrendering control over some aspect of their lives and continue to make decisions in the areas that are off-limits for their Dom

- A submissive re-submits to the Dom at the start of any scene or activity over which the Dom has negotiated authority. Importantly, the submissive retains the choice as to whether or not to submit to the Dom.

Consensual slave

- M/s relationship is based on authority *transfer* (This means that once the person who is to become the slave has, in fact, surrendered personal authority over him/herself to their Master/Owner, they no longer have the personal power to make decisions for him/herself. Thus, a slave would not have the authority to enter into a D/s scene with someone other than their Master/Owner without that Master/Owner's specifically transferring THEIR authority over their own slave to another person.)

- At least in theory, the slave gives up all rights to make personal decisions and becomes the *property* of a Master or Owner.

- The core values are *service* and *obedience*.

- The slave loses the right to say *no* to Master: in its place, slave may say, "Sir, if it pleases you, Sir" to mean: "Master, I really rather would not do that." or "Sir, only if it pleases you, Sir" which is as close to *no* as slave is permitted. (Note: Master has an ethical obligation only to push through an *only if* reply so long as Master thinks that doing so remains in the slave's best interest. Requiring a slave to proceed through an *only if* command on Master's whim violates the basic Master/slave pact on Master's part and represents a contract violation.)

- As slave cannot *red out*, slave thus has accepted their Master's limits and does what is asked of them regardless of their feelings about it. ("What does *liking it* have to do with it?")
- In many cases, a slave will give up their rights to personal property and will continue to work for the benefit of Master's household or business.
- A slave's purpose is to make Master's life easier. In that regard, a slave is expected to know Master's wants and likes to the extent that the slave can take independent action on Master's behalf (proactive rather than reactive; to show initiative as a thinking person)
- If a slave removes their own collar it constitutes withdrawal from the relationship
- May be more interested in taking care of others (service heart) than in being taken care of (*sorts by others* in psychology-speak)
- May very well be a dominant in most other aspects of their life, but have chosen to be submissive to (or simply to serve) one single person

Switch–common use: someone who enjoys being either the Top or the bottom; enjoys giving or receiving physical SM stimulation. Among Leathermen, activity switches are sometimes referred to as *versatile*.

Switch–less common use: someone who is willing to take either the leadership or subordinate role in a relationship depending upon the *chemistry* or *connection* within that particular partner. When used this way, a person is referred to as a **psychological switch**. (Note: while *physical switches* can easily switch within their relationship, *psychological switches* do not. Psychological switches would have relationships wherein their roles are different—dominant in one relationship and subordinate (not necessarily submissive) with the other. This is an advanced and controversial topic and I only touch on it in this book.)

Top: the person *doing* the action.

Top/bottom play: sensation play with SM toys/tools—no psychological dynamic, no power exchange. *Top* and *bottom* are terms that relate to physical action only. The Top spanks the bottom. The Top or the bottom may be a dominant person or a submissive person of either gender. *Top* and *bottom* only describe *roles* while *dominant and submissive* describe relationship behaviors. The decision to Top or to bottom is only a decision of which person wishes to receive sensations that the tools/toys produce when handled by someone who has been properly trained.

Top-space: A state of intense focus and concentration sometimes attained by a Top during particularly intense scenes.

Vanilla: The term used by those of us who practice BDSM sex for those who do not practice BDSM sex. It's not a pejorative term, simply a descriptor. Typical uses: vanilla sex, land of vanillas, etc.

Supplement B: Suggested reading
First, an apology to authors whose works are not listed here. There are so many extraordinarily good books on the market that I've had to force myself to stop listing them, here. These books should only represent a starting point for your further reading.

Books if You're Just Starting Out in BDSM
- *Screw the Roses, Send Me the Thorns: The Romance and Sexual Sorcery of Sadomasochism* by Philip Miller and Molly Devon (The classic guide to sadomasochism that is intended to strip away myth, shame, and fear, about BDSM to reveal truths about this intense form of eroticism.)
- *When Someone You Love is Kinky* by Dossie Easton and Catherine Liszt (VERY helpful for explaining your interest and involvement in BDSM to non-kinky family and friends.)
- *Sensuous Magic, 2 Edition: Your guide to SM for Adventurous Couples* by Patrick Califia (Califia mixes erotic vignettes with practical advice and personal insights to produce a very creative guide to sadomasochism for couples.)
- *Playing Well with Others* by Lee Harrington and Mollena Williams (Interestingly, this book is a marvelous companion to this book that you've been reading. We cover very little ground in common and their material really picks up where this book has left off. And both authors are friends of mine.)
- *The New Topping Book,* by Janet W. Hardy and Dossie Easton (Helps to explain what make someone a "good" dominant, including some of the mental aspects of being a dominant, offers some advice on BDSM play and techniques, and covers the all-important area of safety.
- *The New Bottoming Book,* by Janet W. Hardy and Dossie Easton (The companion to the previously-recommended book, this one is written for submissives/bottoms and deals largely with the mental/emotional aspects of being a submissive, rather than hands-on instructions in techniques and toys.)

Books on the Psychological Aspects of BDSM
- *The Control Book* by Peter Masters (One of my favorite

books: it's about the fine art of taking control of your partner. The processes involve using control, ensuring that you have control, and—importantly—about giving control back once you are done with it. To his vast credit, Masters also discusses how to fix a situation if it goes psychologically wrong.)

- *This Curious Human Phenomenon: An Exploration of Some Uncommonly Explored Aspects of BDSM* by Peter Masters (Masters is one of my heroes. Fabulous author and profound thinker. There is material in this book that you simply won't find addressed by any other author.)
- *Partners in Power: Living in Kinky Relationships* by Jack Rinella (A *must read* before you start a D/s relationship. It addresses the question: "Is it possible to form lasting, healthy, loving relationships that are based on power, control and pain?)
- *The Master's Manual: A Handbook of Erotic Dominance* by Jack Rinella (Another *must read*—particularly if you're starting down the Master/slave path.)

Core Readings for creating/maintaining a Dominant/submissive relationship
- *Leading and Supporting Love* by Chris M. Lyon (Only book in print that describes workable ways to establish and maintain hierarchical relationships that are mutually supportive. Very sophisticated yet easy to read.)

Core Readings for Master/slave structure or theory
- *Master/slave Relations: Handbook of Theory and Practice* by Robert J Rubel (This will provide your best opportunity to get an overall understanding of Master/slave relationships—especially about things to think about before starting one and techniques for maintaining such a structure once you're in one.)
- *Master/slave Relations: Communications 401—the advanced course* by Robert J. Rubel (Out-of-the-box communications book that provides a wide range of work-arounds to often-hidden communication challenges.)
- *Master/slave Relations: Solutions 402—living in harmony* by Robert J. Rubel (A book intended to help you think through

many of the core issues that can come up in authority-based relationships. The book is intended to help you clarify your own values and intentions.)

- *SlaveCraft: Roadmaps for Erotic Servitude—Principles, Skills and Tools* by Guy Baldwin (Profound and masterful book discussing the philosophy and practice of service.
- *Dear Raven and Joshua* Questions and Answers About Master/Slave Relationships by Raven Kaldera and Joshua Tenpenny (Read this before you establish your D/s or M/s relationship: it will save you a world of hurt.)
- *Ask the man who Owns Him* by david stein with David Schachter (Interviews with long-term gay Master/slave couples: demonstrates the wide variety of approaches to hierarchical relationship structures.)
- *Analyzing Performance Problems: Or, You Really Oughta Wanna—How to Figure out Why People Aren't Doing What They Should Be, and What to do About It,* by Robert Mager and Peter Pipe (Another "must read" when developing a training program for your slave.)

Core Readings for Protocols
- *Protocol Handbook for the Leather slave: Handbook of Theory and Practice* by Robert J Rubel (An actual slave's protocol manual, this gives ample examples of protocols that can be modified for your particular relationship.)
- *Real Service* by Joushua Tenpenny and Raven Kladera (A "must read" if you're thinking of preparing a manual of protocols for your slave.)

Books about the Leather Culture
- *Leatherfolk: Radical Sex, People, Politics, and Practice* by Mark Thompson (Great book for developing an understanding of what *Leather* is all about.)
- *The Leatherman's Handbook* by Larry Townsend. (Published in 1972, this was the first book to write out the codes of conduct that the underground Leather scene and SM play that gay Leathermen lived by. This is the basic book on this subject.)

- *Urban Aboriginals* by Geoff Mains (This book explores the spiritual, sexual, emotional, cultural, and physiological aspects that make this "scene" one of the most prominent yet misunderstood subcultures in our society.)
- *Ties That Bind: The SM/Leather/Fetish Erotic Style: Issues, Commentaries and Advice* by Guy Baldwin (A practicing psychologist and one of the most important thinkers on subjects of SM/leather/fetish erotic style, this is a "must read" book covering relationship issues, the Leather community, the SM experience, and personal transformation, as they relate to this form of erotic play).
- *Leathersex: Your guide for the Curious Outsider and the Serious Player* by Joseph Bean (Another of the basic books about Leather by one of the most knowledgeable and lucid writers to tackle the topic.)

Other Books that I Recommend Highly

- *Living M/s: A Book for Masters, slaves, and Their Relationships* by Dan and Dawn Williams (Good friends and a great book for those interested in the realities of living daily in a Master/slave structure)
- *The Ultimate Guide to Kink: BDSM, Role Play and the Erotic Edge* by Tristan Taormino (This is a marvelous collection of seriously sophisticated essays ranging from expert how-to tutorials to thought-provoking essays addressing complex questions about desire, power, and pleasure. The essays are written by extremely well known national presenters who are sexuality and/or BDSM educators.)

Books about Leather Spirituality

- *Sacred Kink* by Lee Harrington
- *It's Not About the Whip: Love, Sex, and Spirituality in the BDSM Scene* by Sensuous Sadie
- *Spiritual Transformation through BDSM* by Sensuous Sadie
- Anything by Raven Kaldera—
  - *Sacred Power, Holy Surrender*
  - *Dark Moon Rising: Pagan BDSM & the Ordeal Path*
  - *The Ethical Psychic Vampire* (This one is about energy play and is in a league of its own.)

Books about Asperger Syndrome— High-functioning Autism

This is a list of books on Asperger Syndrome that I've personally found very helpful.

- *22 Things a Woman Must Know: If She Loves a Man With Asperger's Syndrome* by Rudy Simone
- *Alone Together* by Katrin Bentley
- *The Unwritten Rules of Social Relationships: Decoding Social Mysteries Through the Unique Perspectives of Autism* by Temple Grandin and Sean Barron
- *The Journal of Best Practices: A Memoir of Marriage, Asperger Syndrome, and One Man's Quest to Be a Better Husband* by David Finch

Supplement C: Where to find information
Useful lists
- Of practically every kink known to man—just in case you thought you'd heard it all: *everything2.com/title/ Submissive+BDSM+Play+Partner+Check+List*
- Glossary of BDSM terms: *www.xeromag.com/fvbdglossary. html*

Social networking sites
- *www.FetLife.com*: "Fet," as it is called, is THE go-to source for just about anything these days. It is the "Facebook" for kinksters. There are discussion groups for just about any topic you can think of. It's my first stop for anything I'm researching. (Thanks, John Baku, for creating this Website.)
- See also: *alt.com, slave4master.com,* or *collarme.com,* etc.

Major general information resource sites
- *bannon.com*: the site that is both 100% authoritative and responsible. Race Bannon, author of *Learning The Ropes: A Basic Guide to Safe and Fun BDSM Lovemaking* not only sends you to responsible sites but also provides some guidance about what to be looking for and avoiding when it comes to Internet searches concerning BDSM and Leather.
- HUGE and extremely useful site for all things submissive: *www.submissiveguide.com*
- High quality information: *www.the-iron-gate.com*
- One of the most comprehensive and sophisticated sites I can recommend—particularly for types of play and the psychology of play—belongs to Peter Masters (Sydney, AU). Clever guy. *www.peter-masters.com/wiki/index.php/The_ Control_Book*

Some of my favorite special-interest sites
- Spirituality and BDSM—particularly Leather spirituality: *duskpeterson.com/leatherculture/spirituality/links.htm*
- Sex and sexuality topics—extensive site: *www.sexuality.org/ books.html*

- Leather news and views: *www.leatherati.com/leatherati_issues/2011/09/switzerland-no-more.html*
- Crazy examples of extremely unusual fetishes—with pictures: *http://acidcow.com/pics/51257-crazy-fetishes-20-pics.html*
- Becoming a more poised and polished adult: *http://www.finaltouchschool.net.*

Outstanding sites with lots of kink-related information
- *collarncuffs.com/resources/dokayu.php*
- *www.frugaldomme.com/dangers/*
- *www.idahobdsm.com/articles.html*
- *http://www.drkdesyre.com/meetppl/orgs/orgs.html*

Calendar of events—weekend conferences
- *www.thebdsmeventspage.com/index.html*

Online BDSM education
- *sexedforadults.org* Disclaimer: I'm a member of the faculty for this site. This is a very professional site that offers both fee-based and free classes and webinars, extensive course

National organizations
- *National Coalition for Sexual Freedom* (NCSF): Formed in 1997, NCSF's goal is to fight for sexual freedom and privacy rights for all adults who engage in safe, sane and consensual behavior. *www.ncsfreedom.org*
- *The Woodhull Foundation*: The Woodhull Foundation envisions a world that recognizes sexual freedom as the fundamental human right of all individuals to develop and express their unique sexuality. They support personal autonomy with regard to bodily integrity and expression without societal or governmental interference, coercion, or stigmatization. *www.woodhullalliance.org*
- *The Buckeye Region Anti-Violence Organization* (BRAVO): Founded in 1996, BRAVO assists over 300 clients annually by providing critical services such as crisis intervention, courtroom advocacy, emergency housing, and support services. In addition to client services, BRAVO does extensive

training and prevention education in not only the LGBT community, but also with various service providers and law enforcement around the State of Ohio. *www.bravo-ohio.org*

Safecall Resources

The National Safecall Network: *http://thenationalsafecallnetwork.org*. This is not the place to call if you're in trouble, but it can help from preventing you from getting into trouble in the first place. They have a network of volunteers who will serve as your safecall if you have no one else to serve that function.

Safecall app for your phone: There is now a phone app called Safecall. It is an automatic safecall that you can set up on your smart phone. More info can be seen at *Safecallapp.com*

Supplement D: Acknowledgments

Although I included an "acknowledgements" page at the front of this book, I'd like to add a few people to that list.

I particularly want to thank my partner and Owner, M. Jen Fairfield, for her extensive help and support during the many months that it has taken to complete this work. This book could not possibly be what it now has become without her extensive guidance and profound understanding of BDSM in general and authority-based relationships in particular.

As often as not, Jen influenced and shaped the ideas that now comprise this book. In order to become an expert in this field, she read dozens of books by virtually every authority in this area of expertise in order to find and to pass on to me some of the important supporting information that has rounded out this work. Also, she takes great notes in BDSM classes at weekend conferences.

In addition to helping me with content and flow, Jen made sure that I had the time I needed to write this book—an important gift, considering how hectic our lives are. Without her support at every turn I'd never have completed it. Jen was also responsible for overseeing the layout and cover design of this book.

Other readers: A few of my friends asked to read this book in draft form and agreed to provide critical commentaries. Each and every comment has helped strengthen this work and I thank each of you for your selfless sharing. In alphabetical order, those readers included: Darcy (Austin, Texas); Joan Offerle, Ph.D. (Austin, Texas); Nikita (Calgary, Alberta, Canada); Master Arach (Austin, Texas); Sir William (Eugene, Oregon), and Vickie (Grande Prairie, Alberta, Canada). Each of you made this a better book than it would have been.

Useful insights: I should like to recognize a few people in particular who have either given me particularly useful insights or permitted me to reprint here some of the ideas that they, themselves, have developed. In alphabetical order, this includes:

- Chris_M (a serious thinker and writer about things ethical);
- Geoff W. (Evil_Geoff);
- Gloria McCauley (Executive Director, Buckeye region Anti-Violence Organization,
- Jay Wiseman (author of SM-101);
- lunaKM (owner of SubmissiveGuide.com);
- Maître Pierre and Mistress Catharine (owners of www. BDSMCircle.net);
- Master Arach (who blogs as TheEroticist.com);
- Master JW (an absolutely inspirational original thinker about Master/slave issues);
- Sabrina Santiago, MSW, (in collaboration with The Network/La Red www.tnlr.org and The New England Leather Alliance); and
- Sir Real (Atlanta, GA).

I also thank the many event producers over the years that have invited me to present at their conferences, concurrently exposing me to most of the best thinkers in this field. This book has benefited from that exposure and resulting cross-pollination of ideas.

Supplement E: About the authors

Robet J. Rubel, Ph.D.

Robert Rubel (Dr. Bob), author, educator and photographer is an educational sociologist and researcher by training. He currently has ten books in print and two DVDs (Books: four on Master/slave topics, two on advanced sex techniques, one on fire play, and three erotic art photo books. DVDs: fire play and beginning impact play).

Recipient of the 2008 Pantheon of Leather's Community Choice Award (man), Dr. Bob has been involved in the BDSM and Total Power Exchange (TPE) scene since the summer of 2001, throwing himself into the literature of the field as though it were an academic study. He presents, judges, and sells his books at weekend kink conferences throughout the year.

Now starting in on his 70s, Bob has had three long-term relationships: a 17-year marriage, a 14-year marriage, and a 10-year Owner/property relationship in which after two years his Owner gave him his own slave. The three of them remained together for eight more years. In his current relationship he serves Jen, his Domme.

M. Jen Fairfield

Jen is Dr. Bob's Master. She has extensive experience managing authority-imbalanced relationships. Her D/s experience began in 1992 as she dipped her toe in the water with a nurturing Mommy/boy relationship. Seeking more control than the Mommy/boy relationship could offer, Jen ended that relationship after one year and—following a year of introspection and personal clarification—entered a full-blown D/s relationship that she ran for another 16 years.

Jen found her home in the Leather culture in the fall of 2010 and has embraced her calling as a Leather woman—to live a highly focused life with a partner (or partners) who are willing to hold themselves to exacting moral and ethical standards.

Over the past three years, Jen has been attending conferences and workshops, reading books, and working closely with Dr. Bob, as he has been researching and writing books and making presentations all over the US and Canada. Over the last year, Jen has developed a growing number of presentations that are separate from Bob's.

Publications

All existing and future publications by Robert J. Rubel Ph.D and M. Jen Fairfield can be purchased through Amazon or though our website *www.KinkMastery.com*

Books on Master/slave Relations
- *Master/slave Relations: Handbook of Theory and Practice*
  This book was totally revised and is now available as: Master/slave Mastery: Updated handbook of concepts, approaches, and practices by Robert J. Rubel and M. Jen Fairfield (2014)

- *Protocol Handbook for the Leather slave: Theory and Practice*
  This is the gender-neutral version of *Protocols: Handbook for the Female slave*. More than a book of traditional Leather protocols, this book demonstrates how to use protocols to make your particular relationship magical. This book is intended to suggest protocols that you, yourself, will adapt to your particular structure.

- *Master/slave Relations: Communications 401 – the advanced course*
  All relationships have communication challenges, and many of these challenges are amplified when living in a structured relationship. This book teases out some of communication glitches that are often hard to identify and modify even in vanilla relationships. This book is written specifically for couples living in a D/s or M/s structure where there are certain constraints when speaking with one another.

- *Master/slave Relations: Solutions 402 – living in harmony*
  If you're sensing that one of you is growing apart from the other, if you are concerned that one or more of your *core values* may be different from your partner and you want to work on growing back together, this is your book. It's really a book of *things to think/talk about* that will strengthen your relationship.

Books Other BDSM Topics
- *Flames of Passion: Handbook of Erotic Fire Play* Las Vegas: Nazca Plains, 2006.

SMTech Book+DVD Combinations
- *Fire Play: A Safety Training Course* (70-minute DVD plus 48-page book) Las Vegas: Nazca Plains, 2012
- *Impact Play 101: Building Your Skills* (70-minute DVD plus 48-page book) Las Vegas: Nazca Plains, 2012

Books on Advanced Sexual Practices
- *Squirms, Screams, and Squirts: Handbook for going from great sex to extraordinary sex*
  Most men want to be good lovers. Most men want to please their female partners. Unfortunately, exactly how to please a female lover is a mystery to many men—and good instruction is very difficult to find. In fact, I wrote this book because I was not satisfied with the books that I *could* find on the subject. Here, in this one volume, is absolutely first-rate information about *the who, what, where, when, why,* and *how* of creating an intensely pleasurable sexual experience for a woman.
- *Squirms, Screams, and Squirts: The Workbook*
  This is a companion book to *Squirms, Screams, and Squirts: and is intended to get the two of you talking about areas you seldom discuss even though you've been together forever. There are lots of "fill-in-the-blank" and checklist pages, but the overall intent is to get you thinking differently about sex.*
- *Screams of Pleasure:* Guide for Extraordinary Sex for those with Erectile Dysfunction (Slightly revised version of Squirms, Screams, and Squirts) (2009)

Books of Erotic and Fetish Art
Three books on erotic and fetish photography titled (with an eye towards perverse humor):
- *Parts: The Erotic Photographic Art of Robert J. Rubel, PhD.* Las Vegas: Nazca Plains, 2006.
- *Wholes: The Erotic Photographic Art of Robert J. Rubel, PhD.* Las Vegas: Nazca Plains, 2006.

Publications

- *Holes: The Erotic Photographic Art of Robert J. Rubel, PhD.* Las Vegas: Nazca Plains, 2006.

Edited Publications
Bob served as the Managing Editor of **Power Exchange Magazine** in 2007-2008. Issue Themes
- *Master/slave Relations—male Master*
- *Master/slave Relations—female Master*
- *Bootblacking*
- *FemDomme*
- *Pony Play*
- *Polyamory*
- *Daddy/boy*
- *Leather Spirituality*
- *Pup/Trainer*

In 2007 Bob made a marketing decision and transformed *Power Exchange Magazine* and into a small book format. This series, **Power Exchange Books' Resource Series**, are 100-page books on focused topics of interest to BDSM or Leather folk. The series is about the "why" of what we do, not the "how." Book titles include:
- *Playing with Disabilities*
- *The Art of Slavery edited by salve laura*
  One often hears: "It's easier said than done." This is certainly true of the art of slave service. This is a delightful collection of nine essays written by established slaves who offer readers a glimpse into the world that they have created with their Masters.
- *Protocols: A Variety of Views*
  This is a collection of essays by nine senior Masters or slaves about how they use protocols in their own relationship.
- *Rope, Bondage, and Power*
- *Age Play*

Books by Robert J. Rubel Ph.D. and M. Jen Fairfield
- ***BDSM Mastery–Basics: your guide to play, parties, and scene protocols.***

This is not a book that explains what BDSM is, this is a book that explains what BDSM is all about. This is a book for people who are considering stepping into real time BDSM, and it is also a book for people who have been involved in the community for a while and know enough to appreciate how all the little bits of information they've picked up all nest together.

This book treats the world of BDSM as a culture unto itself and goes a long way to explaining the expectations, rules, and words that are common to this culture.
This book does *not tell you how to use any implements (floggers, canes, etc), but it does explain why in the world you'd want to use such implements.*

- *BDSM Mastery–Relationships: a guide for creating mindful relationships for Dominants and submissives*
This is a book about relationships. Adventuresome relationships. Relationships that are not exactly like *vanilla* relationships—traditional relationships as practiced by the average person you'd meet at a baseball game. BDSM relationships differ in two specific ways: first, they usually involve a power-imbalanced structure (one person is clearly in charge and the other person is clearly following); second, the kind of sex that adventuresome folks practice is, well, *not vanilla.*

Biases though I am, I'd say that if you're in any way involved with BDSM and considering taking a partner, you'll find this book very useful. It can save both D-types and s-types a lot of heartache and anger.

- *Master/slave Mastery: Updated handbook of concepts, approaches, and practices*
This book is the first in a series of books devoted to Master/slave mastery. Yes, I've written other books on Master/slave topics, but that was in the 2006-7 period and I've learned so much since then that this series updates and expands those ideas. This is the first book in this new series, and it's designed to give you a thorough understanding not only the

intricacies of the Master/slave dynamic, but also how vastly different M/s is from D/s. This series of books are designed both to demystify this topic and to give you the tools and knowledge to explore this small sub-culture that lives within the overall BDSM culture.

- ***Master/slave Mastery: Refining the fire—ideas that matter***
In my view, the Master/slave dynamic provides an almost unique opportunity for a like-minded couple to design a magical life for themselves… so long as their purpose and intention is aligned. When you find a strong, visionary leader coupled with a strong supportive follower, quite a bit can happen. However, this formula of interconnected service and support is contrary to the Master/slave dynamic often expressed in fiction. In most M/s fiction, the slave simply does as Master instructs because that's the way it is. The problem with that approach is that by the time the slave is 70, he/she may well feel that their life has been thrown away fulfilling someone else's dream. They may feel sad and bitter.

This book presents many viewpoints on M/s relationships that I have picked up from dozens and dozens of M/s relationship workshops, dozens of books, extensive discussions with hundreds of people who identify with Mastery and slavery, and from personally living in structured M/s relationships since 2003. I have lived as property, as Master, and currently as slave. I am a psychological switch, but you would know that simply from this sentence.

We have a website:
www.KinkMastery.com

On that website, you can see all our books and either order them unsigned through a direct link to Amazon or purchase signed copies through us. There are various purchasing options for the books.

Also, you can buy most (if not all) the books that we recommend through Amazon through our site. This will save you looking them up on Amazon. As we find interesting books to recommend, we list them on the website. Obviously, as this is a printed book, the website list of recommended books is more current than what I provided here.

Actually, the *www.KinkMastery.com* website has a lot more on it than access to our books. There are links to our bi-weekly free Webinars, some of my erotic photography as well as my nature photography, and a place to add yourself to our "notifications" list to receive notices of new books, conference appearances and other bits of news about us.

Again, thanks for purchasing this book; if you ever see us at a conference, please come up and say "hi."

Robert J. Rubel
and
M. Jen Fairfield

Jen and Dr. Bob have partnered for presentations at Leather and BDSM Conferences both in the United States and Canada. They host a bi-monthly webinar called An Evening With Jen and Dr. Bob that covers both power-imbalanced relationship issues and also a range of kinky topics.

Jen and Dr. Bob bring their strengths (and weaknesses) to their work, sharing their life experiences and their passion for education.

You can follow Jen and Bob at www.KinkMastery.com where they share interesting kinky images (that Dr. Bob has taken), resources to aid you on your kinky journey, and ideas you may not have thought of. You'll find a range of (perhaps) new thoughts and ideas that go beyond the World of Kink. You'll also find their presentation calendar and schedule of publication dates for future books.

If you'd like to join their bi-monthly free webinar discussions, you can register at: www.CreativeSexuality.org. Just sign in to the "free online events" tab and click on: "An Evening with Jen and Dr. Bob," and then click on "get e-mailed reminders."

www.KinkMastery.com

Creative Studio

Made in the USA
Monee, IL
17 March 2021